Fabulous hair

Robert Vetica

Fabulous hair

celebrity hairstyling techniques made simple

foreword by salma hayek
and introduction by debra messing

APPLE

First published in the UK in 2009 by
Apple Press
7 Greenland Street
London NW1 0ND
United Kingdom
www.apple-press.com

ISBN-13: 978-1-84543-315-4

10 9 8 7 6 5 4 3 2 1

Text by Robert Vetica
Edited by Ellen Phillips
Cover design by Cristiano Tolot
Book design by Holtz Design
Hair by Robert Vetica, assisted by Aviva Perea
Photography by Alberto Tolot
Fashion styling by Jewels
Cover makeup by Matthew Van Leeuwen
Interior makeup by Robert Jones

Printed and bound in Singapore

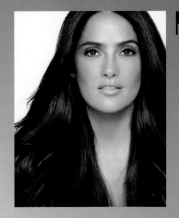

I HAVE HAD THE PRIVILEGE to live a very glamorous life. However, I have found the most amount of joy and beauty in simplicity.

Robert Vetica and I met many years ago when I first moved to Hollywood. As our professional success flourished so did our friendship. I am well aware of his appreciation, respect, and understanding of women. I applaud his commitment to celebrating female creativity and intelligence by writing a book about hair that is not just pretty pictures, but actually teaches women how to become self-sufficient when it comes to their hair.

Robert's simple techniques not only help women achieve their natural hair beauty, but also present high glamour looks that every woman can easily understand and execute.

Many women try to make the most beautiful version of themselves in the most complicated, expensive, and sometimes unhealthy ways. They engage in procedures and trends that often have catastrophic results. In an effort to "fix it," they get further and further away from the original vision.

Robert's book, *Fabulous Hair*, breaks the myth that great hair belongs only to the few women who have access to the experts and expensive products. He connects a woman back to her mane and helps her re-establish a relationship with her hair by going back to basics.

His skillful but uncomplicated approach guides every woman to a clear and basic understanding of her hair and to the tools and techniques she needs to make it look amazing. Robert knows—and shows you—how good you are, how great you can be, and that you can do it yourself!

SALMA HAYEK

Foreword

cont

ents

Robert's GIFT

«YEARS AND YEARS OF WATCHING
AND LEARNING AND ASKING, AND NOW
I CAN WAKE UP IN THE MORNING AND KNOW
I WON'T HAVE A BAD HAIR DAY. IN FACT,
I KNOW I HAVE THE TOOLS TO MAKE MY HAIR
LOOK HEALTHY AND CHIC. EVERY DAY.
AND THAT FEELS GOOD.»

ARTIST. INTERNATIONAL ÜBER HAIRSTYLIST. MASTER.

Robert Vetica is all of these things; he has earned these monikers. And to the few lucky women, like me, who get to call him "friend," he is so much more.

He is a kind heart, a passionate sculptor, a magician, a sorcerer— an "uncle" to my son, a member of our family, a deeply spiritual man who absolutely adores women, and the only man whose presence strips me of all my insecurities, because I know I am in his hands.

Our hair—for better or for worse—has the power to instill in us feelings of confidence, sex appeal, health, and youth. It also has the power to make us want to stay in the house all day, or hide under a hat. It doesn't matter where you are from, or what you do for a living; this is the daily challenge we women face.

When I first started working with Robert over a decade ago, I would sit in his chair at a photo shoot, and watch in amazement as he would—faster than seemed possible—transform my frizzy, dry, puffy hair into something shiny, modern, and feminine that made me feel beautiful. I would always make a date with my husband on those days, knowing I could never replicate what Robert did. (My husband would too soon have his ponytail-wearing wife back, as soon as I washed my hair.) I resigned myself to the fact that for 50 percent of the time, during my non-professional time, I'd look like a frizzball.

But years and years of watching and learning and asking, and now I can wake up in the morning and know I won't have a bad hair day. In fact, I know I have the tools to make my hair look healthy and chic. Every day. And that feels good.

So dig in. I know that Robert would love to help every woman in the world feel empowered and beautiful. This book is his gift to womankind.

DEBRA MESSING

THE ROAD LESS TRAVELLED

Where do I start? How about here: I'm at yet another airport in the world, in Brazil to be exact, and just had a meltdown when I departed the plane and saw the three-hour-long line that would eventually get me through customs and then on to my next plane. Oh, by the way, I have to wait another ten hours to catch that flight. And oh, did I mention that my luggage didn't arrive, didn't even make the plane in L.A.? This is not an uncommon occurrence in my life, and being away from home is just the nature of the biz.

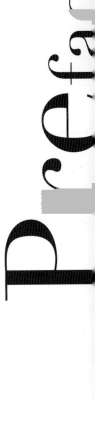

I'M ROBERT VETICA. For three decades, I've been lucky enough to do the work I love, working with incredible people and creating beautiful images for magazines, international salons, the red carpet, the music and advertising industries. I'm one of the lucky few who chose a profession early on and loved it. To this day, I still love what I do.

My work with top models, celebrities, and fashion editors may look glamorous, but I'm still, first and foremost, a hairdresser. I'm one of the working parts of the huge entertainment and fashion industry, and my involvement is part of the publicity machine. Anytime, anywhere, that an actress or a recording artist is promoting their latest hit movie or #1 album, I am one of the people who sell it to you, the public. I am the hair part of that image. We, a team of us, help create the image: hairstylists, makeup artists, photographers, art directors, editors, set designers . . . well, actually a whole slew of people are part of the image-creating team.

And as far as this airport experience goes, well, it's just part of the glamorous lives that you all think we live. I'm not crying anymore. But I have to give you the real deal when it comes right down to it, not the airbrushed version.

How boring would it be if I just started off by telling you how fab it is to be ME, flying around the world from Rome to Paris, Berlin, New York, London, Portugal, Monte Carlo, Tokyo, New Zealand, and then back to L.A., all to blow-dry some gorgeous woman's mane for about one hour. And yes, sometimes that's all the time I spend with them, and then I get on the plane again and fly back to my humble home, where my loving husband and two dogs are waiting with open arms. But you know, that's probably the best part of all of it! Because half the time, it's like I dreamt the whole thing and the only real part is the leaving and the coming home.

These days, I may be a stylist to the stars, but I started small. I went to a small-town beauty school where I learned the basic principles of hairdressing. And I mean I really learned. When you read, you begin with A, B, C. When you sing, you begin with do, re, me. With hair, believe me, there is a step 1, 2, 3.

Proving GROUND:

When I first landed in Hollywood some fourteen years ago,
I came from Milan, Italy. I had been living there on and off for over
ten years. Let's just say that Milan was my high school, university,
and graduate school. I came out of that experience with what
I believe is a doctorate in hair and an eye for photography. It was
there that I honed my skills.

I could never have imagined when I went to Milan that the experience would shape me into the man I am today. At that time, you
were required by fashion law to have European tear sheets in your
portfolio. (Tear sheets in the biz are photographs of your work that
you cut out of magazines, then put them in a book, your portfolio.)

Now the hard part was to get the opportunity to actually work for
the magazine! You had to first have a portfolio so some editor could
look at your work, then book you for his or her next shoot. Once
again, my hard work and luck came into play.

I came to Milan with the guts and passion that only youth can
provide. (Remember that feeling?) And with a genius photographer,
Marco Micheletti, I managed to create a portfolio of photographs
that got some notice, and I landed my first Italian agent. I'll never
forget it.

MILAN

Not that I was exactly hitting the big time. I made absolutely no money, and worked for free most of the time. I can't tell you how I survived, but I did. Anytime I got enough money together, I would buy enough pasta to last a few weeks. And you know, I was happy, really, really happy. Completely crazy, but I was living my passion.

By the end of those ten years, I managed to come back to the States with a portfolio of work to be proud of: covers of every major Italian fashion magazine, as well as amazing images from working directly with some of Italy's top designers like Giorgio Armani and Gianfranco Ferré—fashion shows that at that time were the real deal when it came to runway models.

At the end of my time in Milan, I met my husband and I met sobriety, and I decided to move back to the States. I was ready for a new chapter in my life, and, as the universe would have it, it was at that time that celebrity and fashion collided. I was fresh from Europe and ready for L.A.

But the whole idea of Hollywood freaked me out. I remember my first gig with someone really famous. I was working on her hair for a magazine cover, and I was shaking, literally. I would have to tell myself early on that I was where I was supposed to be, the universe was unfolding as it should, and all I had to do was show up and it would all be OK. (I would actually repeat this mantra over and over, and, no, I am not kidding!)

That's what I mean when I talk about relying on the basics. If it wasn't for keeping it simple and trusting in the basic principles of hairdressing, I wouldn't be here writing this book, and you wouldn't be reading it.

From
HAIRDRESSER
TO HAIR AUTHOR

So I'm writing this book to give back something that has been such a gift to me. To teach you the basic principles of hairdressing. To help make your life just a bit easier. It's truly the one thing that's been missing in my life, sharing my knowledge.

I've been so blessed in my life. Now I feel that it's time to give something back. It's time to get back to my roots, back to the basics. I just can't explain to one more beauty editor how I did Debra Messing's hair for the Emmys or Marion Cotillard's for the Oscars—it just doesn't translate to a paragraph in a magazine.

I remember to this day the loyalty of the women that I used to do when I worked in salons earlier on in my career. Their loyalty was remarkable. Maybe it was that loyalty that gave me the courage to go where I did and to arrive at this point. So it is for them that I find myself back here again. Back to you, to return the favour.

Thank you.

BEAUTY PERSONIFIED

People always ask me who's the most beautiful woman I've ever worked with. Well, that's an impossible question to answer, when, on a day-to-day basis, I have clients like Hilary Swank or Shakira or Eva Longoria, Debra Messing or Annette Bening, or Renée Zellweger, Reese Witherspoon, or Scarlett Johansson. What about Naomi Watts, all those amazing moments for her Oscar press when she was nominated for *21 Grams*? Or Marion Cotillard at her 2008 Oscars? And what about the Judds? Yes, all three of them. Naomi, Wynonna, and Ashley. Where did all that beauty come from? If they could only clone that gene.

Then there is Avril Lavigne. I think the world hasn't even discovered this young woman's beauty yet. And Jennifer Lopez is *really* even more stunning in person, and a love to work with. Then there's Rose McGowan, Anastacia, and Kyra Sedgwick. And Mariah. Mariah Mariah Mariah, AMAZING!

Salma Hayek is beauty personified. I still after, God I don't know, I've stopped counting how many years, never ever get tired of looking at her. She stuns me, and at times, seriously, I'm breathless. She is a dear, dear friend of mine, so maybe I'm biased, but there it is.

My truth is, they *all* are beauty personified, and when we are on set and the magic happens, well, then I understand why I chose the work that I do. I know that I'm not discovering a cure for cancer, and that what I do for a living is a major gift, but you know, here is my truth.

These women, these stars, underneath it all, are women just like you. They have a heart and soul and have joy and pain in their lives. Maybe they don't show it as well, but I understand what it might be like to be in their shoes, to give up their lives for the love of their art. I also understand that they had no idea what a sacrifice they were making. It is quite a sacrifice to give up your personal life for your career, to not be able

to walk out the door without being hounded, to have your body and face and hair and makeup scrutinized by every news outlet in the world. These women, *my* women, my friends, are amazing. They have endured the worst scrutiny imaginable, and endured it with grace.

I have in all these years never met one star that I didn't like, and the ones that I work with on a regular basis, I am comfortable to say, I love.

To you, the women that I love, who have given me such joy on this journey, even the ones that I don't see all the time, thank you for being in my life, for bringing me into yours. I only hope that I've given you a moment of peace, and maybe a laugh or two, not to mention great hair. Know that I get you and I've got your back.

«MASTERING the basics
— *is the secret* —
TO BEAUTIFUL HAIR.»

Part I
THE ESSENTIALS:
Great Hair Starts Here

chapter 1

HAIR
THEN,
NOW, AND
ALWAYS

FROM THE BEGINNING of time, a woman's

hair has always been considered her crowning glory. An old cliché, maybe, but don't you think that it's as true today as it ever was? Think of Eve, with her long, flowing, golden tresses, enticing Adam to eat the apple.

We can't even mention great women of history without thinking of their hair: Cleopatra, Nefertiti, and the other queens and courtiers of Ancient Egypt, who shaved their heads to stay cool in the sultry Egyptian climate, but wore wigs when they went outdoors to protect their heads from the fierce sun, and put on massive, heavily ornamented wigs for state occasions. Joan of Arc, who chopped off her hair to defend her honor. Or let's talk about women through the ages, courtesans and princesses, all with hair so intricately styled that it would take hours to achieve the desired look.

LET'S TALK about wigs in Europe, too. When wigs first came into fashion, in the ultra-fashionable court of the Sun King, Louis XIV of France, in the 1600s, fashion-setters went to great lengths to make the wigs as high as possible, so that the only thing most could afford to use was horse hair. To bulk it up, they filled the inside of the wigs with hay to give it height. Then they started to put perfumed pomades and powder on the wigs to keep the flies and the smell down. Crazy but true! Marie Antoinette, the style diva of her day, wore huge, elaborate wigs that often contained cunning ornaments like birds and boats.

What about more modern style icons? Greta Garbo, Judy Garland, Joan Crawford, Bettie Page, Mae West, Twiggy, Marlene Dietrich, Marilyn Monroe—the list can go on forever. You may remember other things about all of these women, or you may not, but one thing for certain, I'll bet you could tell me their hair color. And I'll bet 75 percent of you could tell me exactly what their signature hairstyle was, too.

There isn't a reference on style, fashion, or cultural history today that doesn't at one point or another mention some aspect of the hairstyles of women of our past. Funny enough, I'll bet none of them did it themselves! They had people like me do it for them.

I would have loved to have gotten my hands on a few of them, just to say I did. But today I get to do the icons of the twenty-first century, and that's not bad! Still, I wonder whether, years from now, other hairdressers like myself will be referring to work that I did—let's say, for example, Renée Zellweger at the Oscars when she wore that amazing yellow vintage dress and her hair was very Veronica Lake. Well, I guess not, because they would refer to Veronica Lake, see what I mean?

« WE REPEAT *the past*
— SO WE can create —
THE PRESENT. »

MY PURPOSE HERE isn't to give you a hair history lesson, though. What I would like to do is to help you, the reader, understand that everything we do in any art form starts at the beginning. We repeat the past so we can create the present, and we do that by learning about the past, the techniques, the principles. Then we repeat them, over and over again, till we can recreate what has already been done, step by step. And then, when we get it, really get it, then and only then can we begin to create something new. It is and always will be this way; there is no other. It is the key that unlocks our creative potential.

Taking Your Hair From
GOOD TO GREAT

I read the same hair tips that you read, and oftentimes, I'm the one giving them. And I ask myself, especially when asked the question from a well-intentioned beauty editor, "How can I explain to this woman in a few short words how I did Marion Cotillard's hair for the 2008 Oscars, and how can a reader like you understand it?"

At times I find that, even when the writer is really trying to get it right, the reader is only going to be more and more confused. I know I get all flustered trying to explain it!

"Come on ladies, section the hair from bottom to top, and then curl the iron downward, and then when you get to the front, start to move it toward your face, and then when you're done with that, pull it all back into a ponytail, and then pin it as if you actually didn't spend the last hour doing what you just read." Right. And once more with feeling!

It's not IKEA, for God's sake. Even trying to follow simple styling directions can send us into a tailspin of distress. Instead, what you need is to understand the basic principles of hairdressing.

Some of you have a real knack for it and others—and something tells me the majority of you—really need help. Otherwise, you wouldn't be buying millions of beauty and fashion magazines to find out the big "how to." Did you know that the beauty and hair tip magazines are some of the most-purchased mags every year?

And I wonder, really wonder, whether they work for you. How can you actually learn how to do your hair from reading a magazine? Sure, these mags can help because they keep you informed of the trends, but the thing is, your education in hairstyling needs to first start with learning the simple, basic techniques.

And you're not the only ones. I can't tell you how many assistants I have had in my life who didn't know how to properly blow-dry hair or use a curling iron. Forget about doing a pin curl or a roller set.

Why do you think the ponytail suddenly came into fashion? Somebody, somewhere, was lazy, or frustrated, or both. Who knows, it could have happened on the runway when the designer gave some hair direction. Then, when the hairdresser was finished, the designer was freaked at what he saw, so he told him to put it all back into a ponytail. Now, I don't know this for sure, but chances are, that's the way it happened. But don't get me wrong—I love a good pony.

In any case, a woman's face is a thing of beauty, and I really think that no bride could ever look more beautiful than when her hair is completely pulled away from her face (minus the ponytail, though).

BACK TO BASICS

When I talk about basic techniques, I mean the basics as in the proper way to set a head of hair, or what direction the hair will go in the wave if you roll this way or that way, or how far from the base of that roller you should drag the hair to set the wave pattern in order to give it the proper direction. Really, this is simple to understand, and that is pretty much what I will do here in my book.

I'm going to teach you basic, simple techniques, not tricks, because there are no tricks when it comes to doing hair. Instead, I'll show you some things that you never thought of before, or maybe you did but never attempted to do them. You will leave this experience with the same knowledge that I have. And better than that, you will learn the same exact steps that I use every day on the job.

I'm not joking here: I do not deviate from the basics. I can't, because I can't afford to. There is no room for mistakes when I go to work; there is too much at stake. For example, at a hair commercial for Clairol or L'Oréal or Neutrogena, do you think for a minute I can afford to explore, as it were, or try something new, like a new product? The answer would be a big fat NO.

And as far as my work on magazines, the red carpet, or anytime I am called upon these days: It's the basic principles of hairdressing, I think, that have set me apart from the others. I have been steadfast with the basics, and it has given me the ability to be fast, yeah, really fast.

Over the years, I have heard many people say, "I can't believe you did this that fast!" In the beginning here in Hollywood, I was so freaked out by the experience that I think I was fast just so I could get the hell out of there. Thank God I had these basics to get me through it.

Once you master these basics—how to take care of your hair, choose the right tools and products, work with style, cut, and color—you can approach great hair with confidence, too. Believe it or not, it all starts with your hair's texture. And that's the subject of my next chapter.

DEFINING YOUR HAIR TEXTURE

chapter 2

CHANGING
TEXTURe

Before we even start talking about what your hair texture is now, I want to remind you that it can change. I mentioned earlier that things like your age and the number of kids you have can affect your hair's texture.

Other things can affect your natural hair texture, too, not even counting perming or colouring your hair, though do they ever! The environment and your personal health can both change your hair texture. Sunlight, pollution, and vitamin deficiencies can all create changes. Humidity can make normally straight hair wavy. And can you say chlorine and salt water?

Hormones also change hair growth and texture. And since your hormones are in major flux during pregnancy, it has a big effect on your hair, both before and after the baby's born. All those prenatal vitamins have a huge effect, causing lots and lots more hair to come in. Then, after the birth, it is not uncommon to lose hair. But eventually, it comes back normally to its original state. And some women's hair stays the same throughout pregnancy; it depends on the individual.

The same thing's true for gray hair. When your hair loses its pigment, the texture may stay the same, or it may coarsen.

But the most damaging things (besides chemotherapy) are serious thyroid problems. Both hypo- and hyperthyroidism can cause dry hair and change hair texture, making the hair finer, and they can also make hair stop growing and increase hair loss.

ARE YOU SURPRISED that I'm starting your journey to great hair by talking about hair texture? Guess what: You'll never have great hair if you don't work with your hair's God-given texture. It's the starting point for everything else.

Now, you may not have a problem with this one. In fact, let me start out by saying that you probably know better than anyone else what your hair texture is. After all, you've been living with it for how many years?! Besides, your hair texture is unique to you, since texture is affected by how old you are, how many kids you have, or how much medicine you have taken or are taking.

In this chapter, I'm going to give you the basics on hair texture. If you follow along, you'll be able to confirm your hair's texture for sure, without confusing the texture with other things, like curliness or how much hair you have. Don't worry: We're going to keep it basic and simple. So let's take a look!

JUST ADD WATER

If you swim a lot in chlorinated pools and don't like wearing a swim cap, the chlorine can make your unprotected hair dry and brittle. To protect it, wet your hair with tap water (or, even better, bottled water) before going into the pool.

Maybe you're a salt-water girl. If you enjoy swimming in the ocean, you may find that the salt water gives your hair great texture. But too much exposure to salt water can have the same effect as chlorine. Before diving into the ocean, wet your hair with tap or bottled water, then add sun protector.

TALKING
TE**X**TURe

FINE

MEDIUM

THICK

I want you to be sure that you really know what your hair texture is, because I will be referring to it quite often throughout the book, especially when discussing style, cut, and product selection. That's because texture determines so many things, from something as seemingly simple as choosing a shampoo or conditioner to something as difficult as understanding how much stress your hair can handle if you decide to colour or perm it. It also determines the types of styling products to choose (as well as the kind of heating elements—such as blow dryers and curling irons—you should use).

Your hair texture really is important! I can't emphasize it enough. I want to be sure that you know your texture. So let's take a closer look at the major types of texture. Compare your hair to the photos and descriptions that follow to find out if your hair's texture is fine, medium, or thick. (Remember, texture isn't about whether your hair's curly, wavy, or straight. What we're really talking about here is strand thickness.)

«TEXTURE IS
— *strand thickness* —
DENSITY IS AMOUNT
OF HAIR.»

Fine Texture

Fine hair is the thinnest strand. It's the most delicate of the three hair types, and is usually light to the touch.

Can you have a lot of hair and still have fine hair texture? Absolutely! Let me clear up some confusion about this: As I said, texture is about strand thickness. It's not about how many strands of hair you have! You can have fine hair with light, medium, or thick density. (Density means how much hair you have per square inch.) Fine hair can also have different wave patterns; it can be curly, wavy, or straight.

Confused? Don't be. It's really simple: If your individual hairs are thin, no matter how many you have, no matter what they're doing in terms of curl, you have fine hair. That doesn't mean your hair is difficult or traumatic or anything. It just means that you have fine hair. End of story! Fine hair is beautiful hair, as we're about to see.

The image on pages 42-43 is a good example of fine, beautiful hair. All I've done is let the hair air-dry naturally, and then I just ran my fingers through it.

ROBERT STYLES
THE STARS

Getting Scarlett Johansson's medium texture, medium density hair ready for one of her premieres is always easy and a blast. She's always ready for something new. To learn how to style the look you see on Scarlett here, refer to Jessica's Third Look on pages 186–187.

Medium Texture

Hair that has a medium texture is heavier than fine-textured hair. But like fine hair, it can be straight, wavy, or curly, and it can sometimes be coarse. It can usually take a lot of abuse, such as irons and colour, and it doesn't really need as much attention as fine hair.

You are really blessed if you have medium hair in any wave pattern. Even if your hair is straight, it can be curled easily and will maintain its wave until it gets wet. Medium-textured hair that's naturally wavy can be straightened with ease, or made curlier just as easily. Out of all three texture types, yours is the easiest to maintain. Lucky girl!

Thick Texture

Wow, to you who have this texture type. You know as well as I do that there is good and bad to having thick hair. The good is obvious: You don't have to do much to your hair for it to look great. You can even just wash and go, assuming you have a good style. And as long as you use the right products, you can really go a few days without washing and/or restyling. Even then, you can get another day out of it by pulling it back into a pony. We love that!

Your hair is what people all say they want. You're so lucky, right?! If they only knew!

Here's the bad side of thick-textured hair (and if you've always wanted thick hair, I hope you're sitting down!): If it's straight, you can't do a thing with it, it won't hold a curl for love or money. If it's wavy, it usually has a mind of its own, and you're forever trying to tame it to do what you want it to do. Not to mention if it's coarse and wavy. And curly thick hair can be a nightmare! It takes forever to straighten, and usually you have to go to a professional to do it. Am I hitting home here, ladies?

Having said all that, we all know how beautiful thick hair can be. Just look at the photo and see for yourself.

Taking Your TEXTURe
ON THE ROAD

Great! Now you really know your hair texture. As you read on, look for references to your texture so you can find the advice I've written specifically for you. Whether I'm talking about style, cut, or product selection, I've made sure each texture type is covered in an easy-to-follow, step-by-step approach. Keep it simple, take the pain out, right?

As I refer to each image and hairstyle in the chapters that follow, I'll discuss the model's hair texture. That way, you can see for yourself what's going to work for your hair.

I just wish I could be there to show you myself! But this is the next best thing. By following the basics I give you in this book, it will make your life easier while showing you how to have great hair.

Now it's time to take a closer look at hair products. Trust me, you don't have to buy a million products to have great-looking hair—you just need to buy the right ones. In the next chapter, I'll show you what's out there and how to choose what you need.

FINE

MEDIUM

THICK

PRODUCT MADNESS

IT'S INSANE, I KNOW. There are more hair products out there than we can ever have the chance to use in our lifetimes. Every other day, there is something new, something better: This one can grow your hair, that one can repair your hair, or add more shine or more volume. More, better, fatter, healthier. And so on.

It would take me ten years to use them all and give you a detailed description of each one. And even if I did, there would be another million, and I would have to start all over again. So here, I will give you the basics, and then you can evaluate any product with confidence, because you'll be able to tell if it's going to work for you or not. As I always say, start with the basics, and if it's not broken, don't fix it.

SHAMPOO SAVVY

Shampoo is a cleanser. It cleans your hair, so when your hair is dirty, you wash it with shampoo. You already know this, so why am I telling you? Because there's something you don't know. Here is the big problem:

The advertising agencies want you to believe that you need to wash your hair every day. They've spent millions of dollars, no wait, billions of dollars convincing you that you absolutely need to wash your hair every single day of your life. And if you don't, you will look and/or smell like a dirty human being and no one will come near you or want you and your whole life will be ruined.

They did such an amazing job of convincing us that we bought the story hook, line, and sinker. I spent the early part of my career convincing my clients of the same deal.

You've been washing your hair every single day, at least once a day. So now you have hair that's unmanageable, dry, and broken. So you abso-lutely need to buy the conditioner that comes with your shampoo or is magically part of the same product, 'cause you need moisture, moisture, moisture. Why? Because you wash your hair so much you take all the natural oils out of it. Your hair is now exactly where the ad firms want it, and you're exactly where they want you: buying more, more, more.

Don't be alarmed. And believe me, you are not alone. Let's talk about what you should be doing instead.

Take Care of Your Hair!

Ever wonder why women of certain cultures have such amazingly healthy-looking hair? These women do not, I repeat, do not wash their hair every day. Never did and never will.

Your hair needs the natural oils that your scalp produces. Those oils are what give your hair luster and strength. By washing your hair every day, you are removing the oil that your body produces and thus destroying whatever chance your hair has to maintain a proper pH. (What is the pH? It's the level of acidity or alkalinity in your hair, scalp, or anything else, for that matter.) And the pH is what it's all about. All we are ever trying to do is maintain the proper pH in our bodies—not too acidic and not too alkaline.

But don't expect your hair to bounce back overnight. Once you decide to listen to me and wash less often, it will take a little while for your hair to return to its natural state. How long? Well, each person will be different. I'd say anywhere from two weeks to six months. The important thing is to do it and give your hair a break.

You will be happier in the long run!

There are some hair types and some women out there who are reading this and saying, well, you're nuts, I go to the gym, I work out, run, do yoga, etc., and I sweat, so my hair has to be washed. The sweat combined with yesterday's styling products makes my hair greasy. I have fine hair and it is just not possible to skip days.

Take it from me, try to just wet your hair, give it a good rinse with just water, and ease up on the styling products. Give this a chance, and I promise, after a time you will find that you have a new head of lustrous, healthy hair.

Listen, ladies, the truth is this: Shampoo has a chemical compound in it that slightly opens up the hair cuticle so the shampoo can get the dirt out. This chemical dries your hair. That squeaky-clean feeling is not what you want! If it was so good for your hair, then why do you grab your bottle of

conditioner two seconds later and attempt to put the moisture back into your hair that you just ripped out? Am I making sense here?!

I'm not going to give you some crazy scientific explanation. Just trust me on this: Washing your hair every day is not a good thing.

The Fun Part: Choosing the Right Shampoo

Most shampoos list a hair texture type on the label, so at least they've made your life a bit easier. In chapter 2, you discovered what kind of hair texture you have. Now you can decide from there what kind of shampoo you need. Read, read, read the product descriptions before you buy! A shampoo for fine hair is exactly that. If you have fine hair, look for that on the label. And if you colour your hair, look for a shampoo for fine, colour-treated hair.

There are some shampoo products that have so much description on their labels, it's insane. Keep it simple. Just because it says you need more of this because you have done this or that, or you live in New York and this shampoo is for hair from New York, don't believe it. Women from New York have the same types of hair as women from Berlin, heat or no heat. We are talking about shampoo and hair type/texture here ladies, remember?

So to recap: Oh, forget it, I'm not going to insult your intelligence here! Just remember the basics. If you need to, go back to the texture guidelines mentioned in chapter 2, find your texture, and take it from there. What I want to do is get your hair back to optimum health. That's why the most important part of choosing the correct shampoo is deciding which hair texture you have and buying a shampoo developed for that hair texture. Then at least begin washing your hair less often and giving it a good rinse more often.

CONDI TION ERS

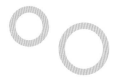

You know, I'm not so sure that everyone needs conditioner. Certainly not the everyday type that we so often use.

As I've already told you, if we shampoo every day as we are told to, so we get that squeaky-clean feeling, then yes, we will need something that coats the hair shaft so it closes the cuticle layer. (Remember that shampoo has a chemical agent in it so it can gently open the hair shaft so the dirt can come out.) The reality is that squeaky sound is not good, it means that the hair is dry.

Think of it this way: The hair is like the shingles on a roof. When the hair is at its optimum, the shingles lie flat. When they are up, the hair is weakened and the cuticle is open. That's why damaged hair seems so dull: the shingles are open, and they don't reflect light. They absorb

MAKING MORE HAIR

One kind of shampoo does more for your hair than just clean it. It's formulated for women who are aging. As you age, you lose hair. Why? It's simple: As your body changes, your hormones change, and one of the things that you notice more than ever is your hair density. (Remember hair density? It's the amount of hair per square inch.)

There are hair products on the market today that really do help promote new hair growth. They work by boosting the sleeping roots that don't want to grow and giving them an extra push. It's like watering a plant: You have to give the plant water weekly to help it grow, and these products work in sort of the same manner. You must continue to use them.

They do not, I repeat, do not grow new hair. What happens as you age is that some roots become tired and go to sleep, some decide not to pass on to their next incarnation, I don't know where they go, but they are not coming home. Others are taking a nap. These hair-growth products find the ones that are just sleeping and wake 'em up. But again, if you stop using them, the roots will go back to sleep and you'll be back where you started from.

The truth is that these products help, but as we all know, as time goes on, nothing is as it was. So don't expect a new head of hair by using them. You can, however, get some significant results that I'm sure you will be happy with.

the light. What we want is for the cuticle to be closed, so the "shingles" lie flat and the light can bounce off the hair, resulting in healthy, shiny hair.

Most shampoos today are gentle. They have to be in order for the big hair-goods companies to sell you the idea of shampooing every day. So the reason I say that I'm not so sure about conditioning every day is simple: If you give your hair a break with the shampoo, then your hair eventually will return to its natural state, and the need for conditioning will be minimal.

Having said this, I am, as a stylist, sort of addicted to leave-in conditioners. I use them as a styling tool as well as a hair moisturizer. We need conditioner to put back moisture, plain and simple, and the women that I work with have their hair pulled, yanked, torn, and destroyed on a day-to-day basis.

So leave-in conditioners have become my best friends, I love them and suggest that you try one. Stay with your favorite product line, I'm certain they make a leave-in, and instead of using a daily moisturizer, try your leave-in. You will be amazed at the results! You might even find that you'll be using fewer styling products.

If you insist on using a daily moisturizer in your regime, then pay attention to the directions. Maybe all you would need is a leave-in on a daily basis and then a good conditioning once a week.

Again, we are talking about hair that is in pretty good shape. (A little colour here and there, not a problem.) But for really damaged hair from colour or perms, you would need some serious hair repair. The truth is that once the hair is damaged to a certain point, there really is nothing you can do other than cutting it. Trust me, it's not worth the time and money to try to bring it back to health. It's just not gonna happen. The only cure I have for that is: Don't go back to the person who did it, and if *you* did it, don't do it again!

LET'S RECAP:

✂ Wash hair less often. Hair maintains its proper pH better when you don't shampoo it every day.

✂ Remember to always read the labels. I still do!

✂ Remember your hair texture and its present condition.

✂ Hair companies have made it easier and easier to choose a conditioner.

✂ But really, ladies, try it my way for a while: Less is more, even when it comes to your hair. Start out by using fewer products and tell me if, after a few months, your hair isn't in better shape.

MY STYLE KIT

When I go to work, I never know what hair situation I'll be facing that day. So making sure I have a styling kit with all the essentials is a given.

I really believe in the products I use. I have never promoted a product that I didn't use. I have used the same styling aids for years. Every once in a while, something new comes along that I find really works and I'll add that to my kit, but the truth is, that's rare.

Today, we are moving toward a new horizon in hair care, a new world with nanotechnology that will change the face of beauty products as we know them. Nano is the ability to make the ingredients so small that they have the ability to really penetrate the hair shaft. Our current products are great, but really they are just dealing with the hair surface. The future in hair care will be astounding for sure!

But you need great hair now. So I've decided to end this product chapter by going over everything that's in my hair kit. These are the wet tools of my trade. (We call them "wet" because all of them have some element of water, and also because they can all be rinsed out with water. For combs, brushes, curling irons, blow dryers, and the like, see the next chapter, Tools of the Trade.)

Kit Essentials

With these basics, you can make a great hair care kit that will get you through any hair challenge. As you'll see, you just need nine products (and maybe less!) to take your hair from good to great.

☐1 SPRAY WATER BOTTLE.

The emphasis here is on the water. Water is and can be used as a hair product. You can reactivate styling products already in your hair by spritzing your hair with water or by spritzing your hands with water and running them through your hair. I also turn to the spray bottle as my mini shampoo bowl when I'm working on a client and don't have the luxury of a beauty salon.

☐2 LEAVE-IN CONDITIONER.

Depending on how a woman's hair feels after I wet it, if it is dry and I have even minimal difficulty in combing through it, I'll either use a spray-on leave-in conditioner, which is usually lighter, or a leave-on cream conditioner, which is heavier. I use the leave-on cream conditioner as a styling agent, because it sort of puts a little weight to the hair and gives better control to whatever set I do.

☐3 HEAT PROTECTOR AND STYLING AGENT ALL IN ONE.

I use this when I'm doing a curling-iron set. It protects the hair from the heat as well as some setting agents that give the hair a better hold. It works wonders really, it's not heavy at all and really helps set the curl.

This is a fairly new product, it's just come out in the last few years, so it might not be available in the brands that you are using. But look around, I'm sure you'll find it further on down the aisle. Or ask your hairdresser. These products come in all price ranges.

Later on, when we get to chapter 9, Hair Styling, I'll refer back to this and you'll be able to see actual examples of when I use it.

☐4 LIQUID SILICONE. Let's give

credit where it's due. Mr. John Frieda made Frizz-Ease a household name. Basically it is silicone for your hair. It really is the last thing you use if your hair is extremely dry. Split ends? Take a small amount, because this stuff is concentrated, and rub your hands together as if you were washing your hands with it. (The rubbing action creates heat and helps the silicone penetrate the hair cuticle.) Then apply it only to the ends of the hair, unless your hair is really, really dry. For extremely dry hair,

START AT THE BACK

When using liquid silicone, always start by applying it to the back of your head. That way, even if you started with too much product, you'll be certain you don't apply too much on the front.

apply it from midway down from your scalp to the ends, smoothing in a downward motion. (Remember the "shingles on a roof" thing I was talking about? You always want to apply any hair product in a downward motion.)

5 **GEL.** I always have some gel on hand. I rarely use it, but I have it with me, because you never know. It's not that cement-type stuff, it's a mild gel that I use primarily to clean up the hairline. Because my work is photographed and filmed, the women I work with have to look perfect. And those fine hairs at the hairline seem to have a mind of their own! Styling creams just don't do it, and because there is a lot of alcohol in most gels, as the gel dries it sort of demands that those hairs stay in place. "Stay down!" I find myself saying from time to time.

So the gel comes in handy at times. Certainly, if I want to sleek someone's hair back into a tight ponytail, a small amount of gel mixed with a small amount of styling cream really does the job. When my friend Anastacia, the American-born, #1 recording artist in Europe, recently got married, we did her hair sort of Grace Kelly meets Evita. I pulled her hair back away from the face, not too tight, but definitely back, and the

mixture of gel and cream did the job. And believe me, we were in Mexico and it was *hot,* but her hair didn't move. That's a good time to use gel as well, in hot weather when you want to keep your hair down.

But I hate curly hair that's gelled. When you touch it, it doesn't feel real. I know a girl that's an art director for a big clothing-store chain, a beautiful girl, Italian I think, with the most amazing hair, long, dark, and curly. But it's stiff as a board. She refused all my suggestions. (But hey, can't win them all!) She gelled her whole head, and although it looked fine from a distance, it was so unnatural to touch. So there is good and bad to gel (and all hair products, really), it just depends when and what you do with them.

LESS IS MORE

When applying any product, always start with smaller amounts. Less is more with hair products!

If you need to, you can always add more later.

6 **SPRAY GEL.** Yes, you see this all over the counters as well, and it really can come in handy. It's like a gel but it's much more watered down, which means it's lighter. I usually use it when I need to do finger waves. That's because it helps me solve my biggest dilemma, the dreaded time crunch.

As a celebrity stylist, about 99 percent of the time, I'm under such time restraints, you would never believe it. For example, in the past, let's say the 1940s and '50s, you would need to use hooded hair dryers to set and style hair. I'm talking those big hooded dryers, the ones you sit under. No one, I mean no one, would sit through that today, even though we are repeating those same classic looks over and over again (with variations, of course). Today, time is not on my side. Granted, we have curling irons that do a reasonably good job, but there is nothing like a wet set under the hair dryer.

Usually we are given two hours to do the whole style transformation. Those hours include hair, makeup, and stylist. On a good day, a stylist is given three hours. Some girls like more time, others less, but basically it's two hours. Now, that means from the time you arrive and set up until you pack up and leave. By the time you park and unpack, a half-hour has passed, and you're now left with one-and-a-half hours. So whatever I can do to make the job go as smoothly and quickly as possible, you'd better believe I do. This is where spray gel is really my friend.

ROBERT STYLES THE STARS

Some stars are blessed with really thick hair, but that blessing can be a curse when every hair must stay in place for the camera. Salma Hayek's hair, for instance. Her hairline is so strong and her hair is so thick and wavy. It's beautiful, really, but if I want that hairline to go from left to right or vice-versa, I use my gel to put it in its place.

Avril Lavigne has a coarse, thick mane as well, and her hairline just wants to stand up and sing on its own. (And boy can that girl sing!) Anyway, I use my gel just on those few hairs that won't listen.

7 STYLING CREAMS AND/OR WAX-TYPE PRODUCTS.

First, let's talk about styling creams. Styling creams add more texture to the hair. What I mean is that clean hair doesn't usually hold a shape well, so whatever your style is, it rarely lasts. To give clean hair the consistency it needs for styling, we need to add gum-based products, and that's what styling creams are.

Your hair texture—fine, medium, or thick—will determine what type of styling cream you use. When you're purchasing a styling cream, buy one you think is too light for you. (Unfortunately, there is no way to test it at the chemist's, so that's why I suggest starting with the lightest. You can always add more!)

A styling cream will make your hair reflect more light, adding shine as well as weight. But be careful, because it can also make your hair too greasy if you use too much. As always, start with the smallest amount.

I use styling creams at the end of my styling. So I start with wet hair, add some spray leave-in conditioner if the hair is dry, and then I blow-dry with no other product. If that's all I'm doing, then I use just a bit of styling cream to give the hair a little weight. Depending on the hair type, I use less or more.

REVIVING GEL

Water reactivates gel. So to freshen up a tight ponytail for the night, remove the pony, spray on a little water, and redo.

《WHEN PURCHASING

styling products
— *buy one you think* —

IS TOO LIGHT. YOU CAN

ALWAYS ADD MORE.》

The wax-based products can be used in a similar manner. But they are much heavier than styling creams and really weigh down the hair. I would never use a wax-based product on fine hair, but will use it on medium coarse and thick hair. However, wax products are great for styling short hairstyles, especially for separations.

I don't like those stick wax products, although men love them. But I hate hair that's stiff! So the wax that I'm talking about is a combo of a styling cream and wax.

Look around the product shelf if your hair is medium coarse or thick; you may find a wax-based product helpful.

As with all styling products, start with a small amount and activate the product by rubbing your hands together. Really work the product in your hands first—it will also help you feel if you have too much product. Many times, because we're always in such a hurry, I put too much in my hands and then end up wiping most of the product off on my pants.

8 **HAIR SPRAY.** There are three types of hair spray, soft-hold, medium-hold, and firm-hold. I use two of them, medium- and firm-hold. I use hair spray in a lot of different ways for many different reasons. First, for the obvious reason, to hold the style. When I do a good blow-dry on, let's say, long hair, I usually set it after with Velcro rollers, and then I use the hair spray as a setting agent.

In my type of work, for hair commercials and print ads for beauty products or for magazine

ROBERT STYLES
THE STARS

I've styled Naomi Watts for different events such as the Golden Globes and film premieres. In fact, for the 2007 Oscars, we did a '20s bob with a finger-waved look. So with my spray hair gel, on blown-smooth, dry hair, I sprayed the top of Naomi's head with spray gel and finger-waved the top and sides, then set them with finger-waving clips. The rest was done with a curling iron. Remember speed! She was having her make-up done as well as her nails, so I had to work fast. Thank the gods that's my trademark! She looked fabulous in record time.

Also, for Marion Cotillard for the 2008 Oscars, where she won Best Actress for *La Vie en Rose*, I gave her a Veronica Lake look with a modern twist, all to one side. That same spray gel was a lifesaver again.

shoots, fly-aways are your enemy. So I spray the hair spray on my hands till my hands are wet with product, and then smooth my palms over the top of the head and along the shape of the style. It's a good trick to spray a bit on your thumb and index finger and finish off the shape around your face. Always use the medium-hold spray for this.

The firm-hold spray is really just for the red carpet. When I need something to not move, then I use firm spray. We really don't need it too much these days, but I always take it along in my kit because my work varies from job to job and I never know when I'll need it.

I recently did a big advertising job for the Equinox chain of gyms, where the models' hair was Barbielike in one shot and eighteenth century *but on crack* in the other. We had fourteen models and that hair needed to stay in place!

So I really don't think that any of you need firm-hold spray in your beauty gear kit, but who knows, next year that could change too. I doubt it though—the '60s hair bouffant isn't coming back for a while. That's not to say that I don't love a good ratted-out beehive when I see one!

In fact, I have to admit that when I travel and see some of you who

don't live by the rules of fashion because you just don't care, well I love that and I appreciate it. Give me Flo any day of the week! Hey, I learned real hairdressing from the Flos of the world: wet set with rollers, under the dryer for forty-five minutes, brush it out and tease the hell out of it, and then comb it into shape. Come back five days later for a re-comb, and then two days after that to start all over again.

That was back in the days when the hair spray was in a bottle attached underneath your station, and you had a sort of hose-type thing with a handle as if you were watering your garden. Out came

«Spray hairspray
ON YOUR HANDS UNTIL YOUR
— *palms are wet,* THEN SMOOTH —
YOUR PALMS OVER THE TOP
OF YOUR HEAD AND ALONG THE SHAPE
OF THE STYLE.»

hair spray like you could never imagine! (I know I got off track here, but it's fun to think about those styles.)

So back to the hair spray: Use it with caution, and never put a match to it! (That's interesting, why would you want to use something that flammable on your head?) Oh, guess what, I forgot, I use only aerosol hair spray, the liquid pump types are just too heavy. Sorry, pump hair spray manufacturers, nice try!

Yikes, I almost forgot my favorite product of all, and I could write a whole chapter on this:

9 **DRY SHAMPOO.** Amazing! There are a few companies that make this product, just go on the Web and search for "dry shampoo." There are several types; one company makes it in colours as well. I love that one, because, since it has some colour in it, you can use it to touch up your roots at the part and the hairline. It's really great (for a perfect example, see page 102).

Let's say you want to freshen up your look after a long day at work. You did your hair in the morning and have to go somewhere that night. As we all know, your hair starts to lose its style as the day goes on. Take the dry shampoo and give your head a good once-over, leave it for a few minutes to let it absorb all the oils from the day, then give it good brush-through. You will be amazed at the results.

The dry shampoo in aerosol form is the one that I use, and that's what I'm talking about here. It also comes in a powder form, but I haven't had the best results with it. It's too heavy, so stay with the aerosol types.

Originally produced for hospital patients who couldn't wash their hair, this product has made a re-emergence into the market. It's even better than before.

Here is what else I use it for: If one of my girls has fine hair, after I'm all finished styling, I give the hair a once-over with the dry shampoo.

Because of its nature, it gives the fine hair body and thickens it.

You may ask why I just don't use a thickening product, as there are so many on the market. Well, the reason is that they seem to have a tendency to leave too much residue and weigh the hair down. They also, in my experience, can be greasy.

You have to remember that I just don't have the luxury to make mistakes. My women depend on me, and the last thing they want is to have to rewash their hair. However, if in fact I did apply too much of something—and it *has* happened—I take out my dry shampoo and it sucks it right up.

Dry shampoo is a wonderful product to have at your disposal. I really freak if I find I've run out, it's that important in my kit.

TRY BEFORE YOU BUY

A lot of beauty supply stores will have samples. Try a few that look right for your hair and see if you like what they do for you.

ROBERT STYLES
THE STARS

Other things that are in my kit really wouldn't be of any help to you, but I will share them with you nonetheless, because you might find it interesting: I carry an assortment of hair glues and removers. These glues are used for hair extensions.

Now that clip-ons have gotten better, and of course it's quicker to clip than it is to glue, women prefer the clip-on hair. However, I used to prefer to use glue, because the idea of hair flying off of someone's head sort of unnerved me. Unfortunately, I can't give you any names here, it would ruin the illusion. So the reality is that I rarely use glue these days, but I carry it anyway because you never know! And the remover is obviously to remove the glue.

One more thing, I use the glue when using lace-front wigs, like when we did Avril Lavigne's "Girlfriend" video, where she played herself three different ways. The lace in the front hairline needed to be glued to give the wig that natural effect.

Later in the book, I will devote a whole chapter to fake hair, hair extensions, wigs, top pieces, etc. You can read all about choosing and wearing them in chapter 7.

Keep It SIMPLe

It would be impossible for me to go through every product that's on the market, there are just too many, and you don't need most of them. Instead, what I wanted to do is show you what I use. And after over thirty years of hairdressing, I have really shortened the list.

I used to carry so much stuff with me. I'm a Virgo, and Virgos are very detail-oriented. I was always afraid that I would need something I didn't have, so I brought everything. Now a little older, a little wiser, I've managed to keep it as simple as possible.

So those are the basics that I bring to work with me, as far as styling products, that is. That's about it; I don't think I left anything out. Oh— always, a bottle of shampoo and conditioner. See, it's pretty simple!

LET'S RECAP:

1. water spray bottle
2. leave-in conditioner
3. heat protector/styling agent
4. liquid silicone
5. gel
6. spray gel

7. styling creams/wax
8. hair spray
9. aerosol dry shampoo
10. shampoo
11. conditioner

And that, ladies, is all that you will need to achieve whatever look you're going for! But wait—what about brushes, combs, curling irons, and so on? I'm glad you asked. In the next chapter, Tools of the Trade, you'll find all of my favourites.

4

tOols OF THE TRADE

EVERYONE HAS a favorite

BRUSH, COMB,

curling iron, blow dryer, and/or rollers. They are like wet products (see chapter 3 for more on those): there are a million to choose from. And they can be purchased, like all hair products, at the chemist's, supermarket, beauty salon, and on television. There are now even store chains devoted solely to these products.

Available in all shapes and sizes, these tools of the trade can either make your life easier or make it a nightmare, depending upon how much you pay or, in my case, how often bad luck strikes.

I remember a moment years ago when I'd just started working with celebrities and I had a pretty important job with one of the famous women of that time. Of course, in my work, every job is important! But anyway, here's what happened: I was using a curling iron, and because I'm such a crazy mess when I work (so unlike the meticulous Virgo type) my stuff was all over the place. I wasn't paying attention to where I was putting the curling iron. I grabbed the iron, did the curl, and went to comb it out, and I couldn't get the comb through her hair! What happened was that, without my noticing, when the iron was lying on the hair station, it was leaning up against one of my plastic brush cases. You guessed it, the plastic melted on the iron, and then that nice hot iron attached the hot, melting plastic to her hair.

OH MY GOD, I can still remember how I was feeling. I freaked to say the least, because the only way to get the comb through that hair was to rip it out. And you know what? That's what I did. I had no other choice. It wasn't that much, maybe two or three hairs, maybe a little more. But boy did I learn a lesson that day! I'm still a bit messy, but I never put an iron to someone's head without looking at the barrel first.

Or how about this one: A few years ago, I was doing the American Music Awards, with one of my favorite clients of my whole career. I absolutely adore this woman, one of the greatest women and talents in our history. I would love to tell you who she is, but let's just say that you all know who she is and leave it at that.

Back to the story. We were running late, I mean really late, and my girl was going to open the show. So she sits in the chair fresh from her shower and we have about forty-five minutes to turn our star into a superstar. I go to start drying her hair and no hot air is coming out of the dryer. Now people, this is one of those expensive, state-of-the-art tourmaline blow dryers. I turn the sucker on, and all that's coming out is cold air!

I was as calm as a Buddhist monk in prayer on the outside, but on the inside, I was completely freaking out. You have no idea, my head was going, "OH $%ˆ&ˆ*%#$@$ GOD, I CAN'T BELIEVE THIS, SOMEBODY HELP ME, WHAT AM I GONNA DO, I HATE MY JOB, THIS IS PAYBACK, OH &%$#@!"

Now, we were in a hotel, and I thought I could just use the hotel dryer, but guess what? It was attached to the wall. So I run to the other room and tell her assistant in a soft, calm voice, "GO GET ME A %$&ˆ&$# DRYER, OH MY GOD, MY DRYER ISN'T WORKING!"

Then I calmly walk back to my girl and start drying her hair with cool air and praying, really, literally

praying that it would dry. I knew that if I could at least get the moisture out, I could use my irons to do the rest. And you know what? It worked! The cool air dried the moisture out of her hair, and the truth is, although it wasn't as fast, I'm sure it was better for her hair.

You know what they say in the entertainment business, the show must go on! And it did. But believe me, the whole experience is something that I will never forget. I now carry two dryers with me at all times!

I'm sure you all have some great story to share about a similar situation. Needless to say, stuff happens, and we learn from it, for sure.

So let's go through my list of tools. In this chapter, I'm going to start with my brushes and combs. Again, these are the things that I carry with me on a day-to-day basis.

COMBs

✂ wide-tooth comb

✂ haircutting comb

✂ rat-tail bone comb

I have a set of three hair combs that I use on the job. One is a wide-tooth comb for combing out wet hair after I've brushed it first. (I use a paddle brush first, before I comb. I'll discuss that next.)

The truth is, I don't even start with a brush or comb until I have felt the hair and know what it feels like. You really can tell what the

proper tool is just by feeling someone's hair. And again, it is rare that I don't start by applying a leave-in conditioner first.

The second comb I use, after the wide-tooth comb, is a haircutting comb, which is longer and more fine-toothed. I don't think that you need one of these to take care of your hair at home!

And the last comb I use is what we call a bone comb (we actually call it a rat-tail bone comb). Where the "bone" part came from, I don't even want to know, but really it's made of wood. (Maybe it was originally made from bone?)

This is a tool that I can't live without. One end is a pretty long comb, and the other is a long, skinny pointed handle. (I guess that's where the "rat-tail" part comes in!) I go through many of these, because I always have one in my back pocket and I break them.

But here's why I think they're a must: Once you've used your wide-tooth comb to comb out the wet ends, you can section your hair easily with the bone comb when you start your styling because the comb is so long, it's easy to maneuver. So you can slice a section in the back, let that drop 'cause that's the section you're going to start with, then pull the rest of your hair up and use the tail part of the bone comb to anchor the undone hair, and repeat.

A bone comb is also great as a styling tool. It doesn't pull out the wave pattern that you just spent an hour doing, but by combing through with this tool, you can separate the hair in a beautiful, natural way. I love this thing and always feel lost without it.

START AT THE ENDS

Never start at the scalp when brushing or combing wet hair! Because hair as it grows becomes weaker from mid-length to the ends, it's best to start at the ends with a wide-tooth comb to detangle. Remember, we might have applied a leave-in conditioner first, so give that a second to do its job, then start at the ends to comb, graduating to the middle, then closer to the scalp. Once that is done, you can turn the comb around, if in fact you have the type of comb that has wide teeth and fine teeth on the same comb, and proceed to comb through again.

See, the whole idea is to close the hair cuticle. (Remember the shingles on the roof from chapter 3? Well, this is what we are doing.) It's important to close the hair shaft so that you're protecting your hair from the heat you are about to apply. It also promotes shine. That's because, if the cuticle is open, the light is absorbed, but when it's closed, it reflects light. Makes sense, right?

BRUSHES

- ✄ flat, natural-bristle paddle brush

- ✄ oval boar-bristle brush

- ✄ three different-sized round brushes: small, medium, and large

- ✄ last but not least, my teasing brush

First, let's talk about the flat paddle brush. I like to start with a paddle brush on wet hair, and I only use 100 percent boar bristle. I have tried everything, and I know other people who use plastic brushes when combing out, but for me, it's only the natural-bristle brushes that do it right. I find that plastic or even the combination of both cause static, and it's the last thing I need, so I stay away from them. You can find these brushes anywhere. Mine is flat and oval.

I use this brush when I first start to work, too. If someone sits in my chair, usually with dry hair, I first brush their hair, and I use this brush to do it. Besides the initial brushing, I use this when I need to give the hair a healthy brushing. Sometimes when I've curled too much, it helps relax that curl. I've found that, after I've been working on the hair for a while, a bit of leave-in conditioner and a good brushing help bring it back to life.

ROBERT STYLES
THE STARS

When I borrow or innovate on a style from the past, which often involves setting hair, it really requires that after the set, I give it a good brushing. I recently did Eva Longoria for an event in Germany, as her mane man, Ken Pavis, was not available. She was being honored for her career and she was wearing this amazing, glamorous gown—very Old Hollywood. So for Eva, young and stunning, I did what I would call a "Rita Hayworth meets Eva" style. A set hairstyle like this needs a healthy brushing afterward, and it's a perfect example of a time you need a flat paddle brush. You just have to have one!

The second brush I use is my favourite, favourite brush of all time, the amazing oval boar-bristle brush that I got from Japan. I know you can't go to Japan to get it, but fear not, I see that it's been copied, so it's out there in your local beauty-supply and chemist's. Because of its shape, this brush allows you to grab the hair at the point of the oval, so you can get really close to the root. As a result, you can get a better grip on the hair, and that means you're not constantly turning and turning your brush till you get cramps in your hands.

This brush enables you to do smooth hair like a breeze, and it's great for fuller hair as well. You can manipulate the hair so much better. And here's a bonus: This brush is longer, it's not your typical 3- or 4-inch (7.5 or 10 cm) brush, it's 6 inches (15 cm) long, so you can dry more hair at a time. Can you tell I love this thing?!

Now, the other three brushes in various sizes are your normal round brushes. I do have a few metal round brushes, as well as the natural-bristle ones. Sometimes I find that the metal round brush is good for thicker, coarse hair. If you have that type of hair, then you can use the metal ones, but if you have fine- or even medium-textured, or dry or sensitive hair, then please, stay away from metal brushes! These brushes, combined with the heat of the blow dryer, can cause serious damage to hair if not used properly. So generally speaking, I would proceed with caution with the metal brushes.

One of the other problems with metal is that, since it is easier to grab hair with a metal brush, women become used to its easiness, but then don't understand why, after they've used one for a while, their hair is damaged and brittle. So easier is not necessarily better!

Next up is my wonderful little teasing brush that I bought at the supermarket. Come on, you know the one I mean! You've seen them at your grandma's, or your Aunt Betsy has one, or maybe you've seen them at the grocery or chemist's on the shelf next to the other 4,000 hair products and accessories. Even if you haven't, all you need to do is look at the photo below!

«FOR A glamorous evening LOOK A LA BRIGITTE BARDOT, — *a teasing brush* IS THE TOOL OF CHOICE. — LIFT YOUR HAIR UP AT THE CROWN, PUSH IT DOWN FROM THE MIDDLE OF THE STRAND, AND REPEAT. *Ooh la la!*»

This little baby is the brush of all teasing brushes. It's small and skinny, with plastic teeth to give you maximum teasing capability. (Sounds important, right?) In all seriousness, this type of brush has been around for I don't know how long, and I remember it from the time I first started working with hair.

I use it for the obvious, to tease hair. And I also use it when I need to give that bump at the crown, you know the one I'm talking about, that Brigitte Bardot look, the one you're looking for to give you that evening look, that little bit of something extra special.

Well, to get that look, you take this brush and lift the crown section of your hair, hold that section up high, then take this baby and start at the middle of the hair and push down, and repeat. It also creates a beautiful smoothness after teasing. Believe me, this is *the* brush, and I think it's really, really inexpensive, actually, I know it is!

Anyway, I guess I lied when I said earlier that I have no plastic brushes in my kit, because this is the one and only one. I will use it later on in the book to show you when it's useful, so you can try it yourself.

So there you have it: Big famous fabulous Hollywood hairdresser that only carries these few basic combs and brushes in his kit:

1. three combs: wide-tooth, haircutting, and rat-tail bone

2. one flat, natural-bristle paddle brush

3. one oval boar-bristle brush

4. three round brushes: small, medium, and large

5. one teasing brush

Believe me when I tell you I've got this down to a science!

Dryers and IRONS

Now we get to talk about the electricals. Those big, bad, scary blow dryers that blow up in your face, and those scary, freaky irons that never seem to do what you want them to do.

Dryers

There are all kinds, aren't there? I guess it depends on your price range, but basically, I think that you get what you pay for. Don't expect a £15 blow dryer to do the same job that, let's say, a £30 dryer will, or, for that matter, a £100 dryer.

DON'T NUZZLE YOUR NOZZLE!

Be careful with the nozzle of your dryer. Some of them come with a metal nozzle. This metal nozzle goes on the end of the dryer to direct the heat where you want it. It's good really, because it makes drying hair easier. But if you have a dryer with a metal nozzle, be careful not to touch your hair with that thing! It can get really, really hot and it can damage your hair. You're right, a curling iron is metal, too, but when you use your iron, it's for shorter periods of time, while you use the dryer over and over again. So that nozzle is like a weapon on your hair. I never touch the hair with it, I only use it to direct the heat. After all, that is what it's made for. And I recommend that you use only plastic nozzles.

Even I think spending £100 for a dryer is a bit crazy. But I have one, because companies give them to me so that my fabulous, famous celebrity clients will see them and want one. So then I give my client one, and then the publicists from the company call the magazines, and they print that so-and-so uses this fabulous blow dryer, in the hope that you'll go out and buy one. Yes, that's the way it works and why not, you're the consumer and you do want the best and the newest, so it all sort of makes sense, I guess! No doubt, I will probably design my own one day. So don't be surprised if you see my name on one!

Of course, this fast-moving publicity machine was not what I had envisioned when I first came to Hollywood. I didn't realize then what I know now, that my clients help sell blow dryers, but hey, why fight it, it is what it is. (Wow, I've gone off on a rampant verbal assault on the publicity machine that I am a part of, but that's the way I feel.)

So even though I have the best blow dryer, the one that costs a fortune, and I get it for free, if you don't have £100 lying around, don't sweat it. They blow out just the same as the ones at the chemist's. (Yeah, it's true, I already told you about the incident at the American Music Awards.) So choose one that fits your price range and is comfortable to handle. As for watts versus volts and all that other stuff, I really never pay much attention. I like lightweight dryers for the obvious reason: It makes my life easier. I think that weight and size—along with price—is what you're looking or here.

Irons

Moving on, let's talk about irons, as in curling irons. Now this is where everyone has a different theory. I would suggest to you that you use the irons that have a spring action on the handle. The other ones have a manual handle and are called marcel irons.

Marcel irons are in my opinion good for pros only. It's already enough for you to try to use this hot electrical rod on its own. So stay away from the marcel type, unless you decide to remove the handle so you're left with just the rod. Obviously, unless you simply enjoy dismantling electrical devices, the spring-action rods are the way to go if you're doing your own hair!

Curling irons range in size from ¾-to 1 ½-inch (19 to 38 mm) barrels. There are some smaller and some bigger ones, but these are the ones you'll find in stores. I carry all four sizes—¾, 1, 1 ¼, and 1 ½ inch (19, 25, 32, and 38 cm)—in my kit. This is all I carry as far as curling irons.

MARCEL OR MARCEL?

Believe it or not, there's some controversy surrounding the inventor of the marcel iron. One contender is the inventor Marcel Grateau, who some experts think invented the marcel iron in France in 1875. But others credit the renowned Parisian hairdresser Monsieur François Marcel, who was also famous for creating the Flapper-style wave. M. Marcel patented the curling iron in 1927, so it looks like Monsieur Grateau lost out on this one, even if he was the original inventor.

Later on in the book, in chapter 9, I'll explain to you how to use curling irons. I know that this part of hairstyling is a nightmare for some of you, and I will show you step-by-step how to achieve the look and style you are going for, so be patient with me. Remember, all we are doing right now is getting you and your hair in working order so your life will be easier and the fear of styling your hair will be removed. And to do that, you need to remove all the unnecessary elements that are in your way now.

Like I've said before and will continue to repeat throughout this book, I have no room in my professional life to make mistakes or try so-called "new and improved" items. I don't think you do, either. So I've learned to keep it basic and simple, and that's what I'm doing for you. I want to give you the knowledge that I have learned in three decades of hairstyling to make your life easier.

Although I carry four sizes of curling irons, I'm sure that you will only need two in your lifetime. Depending on your wave pattern, you can choose which ones suit you.

Let's say, for example, that you have curly hair. You will no doubt choose the size of your curl, so when you are wearing your hair natural for that day, and you just need to touch up those curls that have a mind of their own, you'll use the size of iron that matches your natural curls. (I know that you who have that curl know exactly what I mean!) But if you want to go for a smooth, wavy look, you may want a curling iron with a larger barrel.

As for you women with straight hair, you might be tempted to think that a big-barreled curling iron is the one for you. But if you've tried one, you'll have discovered that the curl just doesn't hold like you want, and you'll blame your hair, thinking that it just doesn't hold the wave pattern that you put in. Well, maybe the problem is that you used an iron with too big a barrel. I always make a tighter curl, and the reason for that is that the curl always drops.

You're right, it depends on the hair. Fine hair *will* take a curl and hold it, but even then, you may want to use a smaller iron. If it's too tight, you can always run your blow dryer to loosen it up. So I always tend to go smaller.

«I've learned TO KEEP IT
— *basic* AND *simple*, —
AND THAT'S WHAT I'M DOING
FOR YOU.»

I only use the big curling iron when I'm going to set someone's hair in rollers. Like when I'm doing that full, free, and easy hairstyle that looks windblown and has just a hint of wave. To get the look, I use Velcro rollers. I do this by sectioning the hair, starting at the top of the head. Section by section, I use the 1 ½-inch (38 mm) iron to heat up the hair. Then I wrap the hair around the iron from end to root, wait a few seconds, remove the iron, and put it down. (Yes, even I have to do that, there are no tricks, you only have two hands.) Then I take the biggest roller I have and wrap it around the hair and clip.

The whole process takes about twenty minutes, but the result is full, sexy hair. This is because heat breaks down the molecular structure of hair, so as it cools, it reforms to the curl of the roller.

I also spray the hair with the heat protector first and then, after it's all set, I give it a once-over with some hair spray. Even then, sometimes, it can be a little tight. So I take my blow dryer, and with my hands only, apply heat from the dryer and move my fingers through, loosening up the set.

These are just a few styles that you can achieve when using the tools properly.

WET-TO-DRY IRONS

I don't know if you like the sound of your hair sizzling, but that's what it will sound like if you use a wet-to-dry iron. Most people don't like it. I like to use it if the hair is 70 percent dry. If I dry the hair quickly but some moisture is still in it, then using this iron is good; it won't damage your hair, but still gives it the style I want.

Flat Irons

Okay, back to the tools. You have your blow dryer, and now you have your irons (curling irons, that is). So now we can talk about the flat irons. Again, there are a million of 'em. I used to carry every width that was made. (Remember earlier on, when I told you the fear that used to overwhelm me, so I always wanted to be prepared for any-thing.) Now things have calmed down a lot and I realize how crazy it was to carry around all that stuff, so I keep it to a minimum. I really only carry one flat iron. Just one, and it is all I need, it is lightweight and it's thin so it can get real close to the roots.

Now, this is also a time that I think that you need to choose for yourself what works best for you. If you have thick, curly or wavy hair, you no doubt want a flat iron that has more girth to it. Those of you who have this type of hair know what I'm talking about, you gotta take that hair and demand that it listen, and for this you need a flat iron with some spirit. Come on, you all know

what I'm talking about, so choose the flat iron that makes sense for your hair type. I can't imagine that you would need more than one.

Do we need to talk about metal versus ceramic versus titanium flat irons? Titanium flat irons are definitely the way to go. Metal irons are heavier, tend to stay too cold or get too hot, and often snag the hair on their plates. Ouch!!! Ceramic irons are a bit better in that they allow the hair to roll off of the plates more easily, so your hair won't get snagged, and they emit negative ions that help close the hair's cuticle layer, sealing in the hair's natural moisture and creating smooth, silky, straight hair. (We're back to those shingles on the roof again.)

But technology has now moved us another step forward, to titanium irons. Titanium plates not only produce tons of negative ions, but destroy any bacteria lurking in your hair. These irons also have special internalized heating

elements that consist of wafer-thin layers of pure ceramic plates, which are computer-designed for precision heat control. These exceptional features produce amazing results.

So there you have it. These are your electrical hairstyling needs.

Oh shoot, forgot about the hot rollers! Yes, they are out there, and they do work when you need a certain style. They also are great for a certain hair type, and when used properly, they can make your life a bit easier. For example, a styled, glam look, perfect for a hot roller set. I'll show you later on, in chapter 9, what I mean. But geez, someone needs to make hot rollers that have bigger rollers, right?

The simple truth is that, with any of these tools, from combs through the electrical appliances, you need to choose properly and remember that these tools aren't gonna last forever. They do tend to have a short lifespan, so remember that when you purchase them.

So now we've covered the basics. But what about the accessories? Funny you should mention those. They're the subject of the next chapter.

WATCH THAT IRON!

Today, the market has produced irons that can go up to 400°F (200°C). The hotter the iron, the less time it should be in contact with the hair shaft. Hotter irons do the same job in a shorter time.

SIGNATURE STYLING TOOLS

Recently, I have decided to launch a product of my own. It has become clear to me that I just wasn't getting the performance I needed from my irons and blow dryers. Then about a year ago, before I started writing this book, I met Jerome Miglori, an amazingly talented man who has designed the most innovative, state-of-the-art products under the Linea-Pro logo. (The Linea-Pro Professional Titanium flat iron, for example, is the longest, sleekest, thinnest flat iron ever made, featuring a signature digital remote control and computerized temperature guide.)

Jerome Miglori is a revolutionary in the hair industry. He and his team, through the Linea-Pro line, are moving our industry into new frontiers, and I am proud to partner with them in creating a signature line. Look for Vetica for Linea-Pro products in major US department stores beginning in 2009, as well as a more affordable line debuting in 2010.

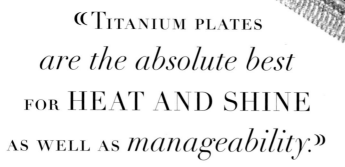

《Titanium plates *are the absolute best* for Heat and Shine as well as *manageability.*》

«Special effects LIKE
— colour AND *hair extensions* —
ARE JUST WHAT YOU NEED
TO GIVE YOUR HAIR
A LITTLE SOMETHING SPECIAL.»

Part II
SPECIAL EFFECTS:
Get Red-Carpet Ready

ACCES
SORIES

chapter 5

RIBBONS
AND BOWS, bobby pins, hair pins,

hair clips, barrettes, rubber bands, elastic bands, head bands, hair bands, and every possible combination! It's astounding. And there are great hair goods companies that make all this stuff. It's just mind-boggling when you see it all together, but for me it's like being a kid in the candy store. I love me some hair goodies!

I can't possibly go over every single item on that store shelf, but what I can do, as I promised, is to tell you what I carry with me every day to make my life easy.

Again, I have had years of practice to keep this to a bare minimum.

Do you remember in the beginning of this book, I told you about flying around the world to work with someone for just an hour? Well, I gotta have at least the bare essentials, right? I mean, God forbid I should show up in London on a Sunday afternoon to work Sunday night, and my girl wants to wear her hair back in a chignon and I don't have the proper elastic bands. Or if she wants to wear her hair half up and I need a barrette to pull the top half up and I don't want the bobby pins to show. And it is Sunday and the stores are closed, and you know what? The truth is, you don't have the option to say, sorry, we can't do that because I don't have the right accessories! So I carry a little of everything with me.

I know it sounds crazy, but you would be surprised what I carry in my little bag!

Kit Essentials

Let's talk about what you need in your own kit. These are the accessories you simply *have* to have: elastic bands, bobby pins and hairpins, hair clips and barrettes, and a giant hair clip.

1 **ELASTIC BANDS.** These are the type without metal. You know you've seen them, and for God's sake, don't buy the elastic bands with metal. And you do know why: You can rip your hair out with that metal, and I know that you have.

So these elastics come in black, white, brown, and clear. You can buy them all together, and that's a done deal for me. I always keep them on hand, not just for pony-tails but for any sort of updo I need to do. (In chapter 9, the styling chapter, I'll explain when and how.)

2 **BOBBY PINS AND HAIRPINS.** Both can be used to anchor the hair. Use bobbies to secure and hairpins to secure and finish. Be sure to match the colour of the bobby pins to your own hair colour. And remember that there are different types of bobby pins for different types of hair. Again, I will explain the how-to stuff later, right now I just want to tell you what I carry with me and what I think you need to have in your own hair kit.

3 **HAIR CLIPS AND BARRETTES.** You can buy these six to a pack, also in assorted colours and finishes. I keep it simple and elegant, because when I use them, it's usually for a red-carpet event, and elegant seems to go with anything, so they are either tortoiseshell or black plastic. I also keep them in metals like gold and silver, which are good for some of my younger clients when they want to pull the front top section of their hair off their face.

4 **GIANT HAIR CLIP.** This one's for you, it wouldn't be fair if I didn't insist that you have one of these in your kit. You will need it to assist you in styling your hair on your own.

Later, I will show you exact techniques, and this hair clip will be like your assistant. You will use this clip as a tool, but you will buy it in the accessory department at the store.

Now, when purchasing your clip, remember your hair texture. Some of these are like giant tiger claws and make no sense if they're too big for the amount of hair you have, so choose carefully. I don't have one because I use that big bone comb (remember it from chapter 4?), and maybe that will work for you, too. I don't know, but I'll show you how to use both, and then you can decide.

EX TR AS

*Special thanks to Jennifer Behr at www.jenniferbehr.com for providing the incredible accessories featured in these pages.

I DON'T KNOW HOW CREATIVE you want to be, but there a couple of other items in the accessory department that I carry with me that might be of interest to you.

One would be finger waving clips. I don't use them that often, usually for a magazine shoot when I want to do quick finger waves. I have also used them on the red carpet for a Roaring Twenties-inspired look. I did that on Naomi Watts for the SAG Awards when she was nominated for *21 Grams*.

They are really easy to use and make finger waving easy. I'll show you in chapter 9, the styling chapter.

The Wig Cap

The other item is for women with thick, wavy hair or thick, short hair. It's a wig cap. Made of nylon-type hosiery material, this wig cap is great when you have unruly hair and you want to keep your hair flat to the head.

You know how sometimes when you just washed your hair and you have finished your styling, you look in the mirror and it's just a bit too puffy? Well, some of you would then take out one of your styling products and apply it, then find out that all you've done is make your hair greasy and lifeless.

Instead, brush your hair off your face and/or in the direction of the part you made and put on the wig cap. Because the cap is made of nylon and is meant to breathe, you can then spray some hair spray right through the cap. Leave the cap on your head for as long as you can (no doubt, you have yet to do your makeup anyway). When you're finished, you'll find that your hair—after you remove the wig cap, of course!—is nice and flat. It's great for the straighter, sleeker looks.

EXTRAS

Wearing a Wig Cap, Step by Step

1. Put hair in a high ponytail on top of head.

2. Place stocking wig cap on head.

3. Cut a hole in the top of the cap and pull ponytail through.

4. Take the ponytail band off.

5. Tuck the length of the hair back into the cap (through the hole opening).

6. Make a knot to close the hole.

7. Distribute the hair under the cap, pushing it around underneath the cap so that it lies flat to the head as much as possible.

8. Make sure the wig cap is behind the ears.

9. Tuck hair underneath the cap on the bottom.

10. Secure hair with a bobby pin in the back above the nape.

11. Place bobby pins in a vertical direction at the temple to secure the wig cap. Make sure that the pin doesn't move in same direction as the hair is moving, because it will not hold it as securely as a pin that crosses the hair perpendicularly.

NOW YOUR KIT'S COMPLETE.
You have the right products, tools, and accessories. It's time to get serious about one of the biggest challenges women face when it comes to hair: colour. In the next chapter, I'll tell you how to (finally!) get it right.

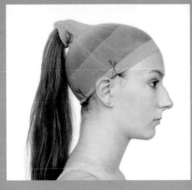

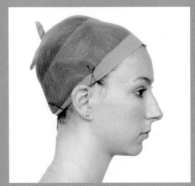

6

COLour,
as in HAIR'
DYES,
HIGHLIGHTS,'
and HAIR's
TINTS

COLOR

This could be a whole book in itself. In fact, the more I thought about this chapter, the more I realized that it really is a book in itself, and so I decided to stay true to my original idea, to stay as simple and basic as possible.

I have spent a good part of my earlier career as a hair colourist as well as a stylist; in fact, I remember carrying the colour around with me as well as all my other equipment.

Remember Salma Hayek early on, when she first arrived on the Hollywood scene? I'm the one who added those beautiful warm tones to that gorgeous Latin hair. What a job that was!

Or how about Wynonna Judd? Now tell me, what's the second thing you think about when you think of Wy? Well, first, we all know it's that unbelievable voice. But next? That amazing fiery hair colour.

Remember the Kmart commercials that Wynonna and her mum Naomi did? That was the first time I met her, and I had to colour her hair, in Nashville. Try to imagine for a second if you were in my shoes and were hired to do Wynonna Judd's hair! Honey, seriously, there is nobody—and I repeat, nobody—that had that hair colour. I was a nervous wreck, I remember waiting for her in a salon that production had found for me to do my magic. I had every concoction of red with me that you can imagine. Yes, I had her formula from her other hairdresser, but still, this is Wynonna, and yes, she is as amazing in person as you think she is!

SO ALL I CAN tell you is that finally, she arrives around 10 p.m. that is, and here I am, so stinkin' nervous, and Wynonna walks through the door holding the most beautiful cupcake I have ever seen. She hands me this work of art, then grabs me and gives me the most sincere hug, and well, that was it. That was a long time ago and many hair colour experiences since. I did her colour, and to this day, Wynonna Judd remains my dear, sweet friend.

Why am I telling you all this? Besides the fact that I want to help you understand the world I work in, I need you to know that there are people out there that really do know colour, like your hairdresser who does your colour, even though the big famous salons have pulled away from the hairdresser doing cutting and styling and colour because it just doesn't work out financially in the long run. (See what I mean about changing times?) Now they are specialized.

I owned a colour business at one point. I was (not on paper) the distributor of a colour company called Renbow International, and we distributed to the Northwest.

I taught many colour classes to thousands of hairdressers, the kind of hairdressers who do everything.

What is this specialty stuff?! You go to this one to colour your hair, and that one to have your hair cut and this one for your dry and, finally, that one for your set?! I get it, I understand it, it's about money, I know, and I'm not here to tell hairdressers how to run their businesses. But if you are a hairdresser and you are reading this, please, for the sake of your client and your profession, have some knowledge about colour.

You know what, colour is a blast. It is the one thing that can really spice up your look. And it's easy, seriously, even if you're doing it yourself. I'm gonna help you take the fear out of colour, and believe me, it is only fear that makes the difference between a good colourist and a not-so-good one.

EVERYONE NEEDS COLOUR

When I worked in a salon, many years ago, I would recommend colour to all my clients. Really, that's the truth. I believe that even if you just add the same colour or tint that you already have, meaning the colour that's naturally on your head, it will give your hair some new dimension.

Just by adding the same colour, you can brighten up a dull brown or a mousey blonde. For example, if you are an 8-level blonde, you can color your hair an 8g, which is a gold blonde. What it will do is add warmth and texture. It will also plump up your hair a bit, and in some cases make it feel thicker and more alive.

GOING
TO
THE PROs

I live in Southern California and work in Hollywood, land of the perpetual blonde. Everyone is blonde, and you know what? They do a damn good job of it here.

That's not to say that I think everyone should be blonde, I don't. Some women are amazing blondes and others, well, let's just say that blonde is not for everyone.

Blonde is not as easy to achieve as it may seem, either. And usually, it takes a professional to do it the right way. That is my Blonde Rule #1: If you want the best, then go to the best, go to a professional. Even my mum's hairdresser, Firma, can do colour, so there is no excuse!

I'll let you in on a little secret. Well, actually, this is a big secret: If you are on a budget, find a beauty school near you. Every beauty school in the country needs hair clients, and every school has a trained teacher on staff that oversees every client that comes through the door. Usually on Fridays and Saturdays, they actually run a salon, and so for a small fee, you can have your hair coloured professionally. Even though the student is actually applying the colour, they are watched over by the teacher. So if you have a hard time doing the back of your head, or maybe your hair is too long, or maybe you just want to be pampered, then go do some volunteer work and be a client for a student in a beauty school. Everybody wins. Hey, you never know, you might meet a "me" in that school!

So let me get this out of the way. If you have any doubts about colouring your own hair, please please please, go to your salon. In the end, it really is not worth the headache (or hairache) to do a bad job at home. But if you are a little adventurous and/or find that you're kind of handy, then here is a colouring guide for you. Yes, you can use store-bought colour to cover your gray or to add highlights or maybe to just give your hair a little something special.

CHOOSING YOUR COLOuR

First things first: Look at the colour on the box! But here's the secret: What you see on the box is not usually what you get. Why? Because this colour on the box was put on hair that was previously lightened!!!

Get it? In other words, that colour was applied to bleached, dyed hair, tinted hair, whatever you want to call it. (I love that they don't want to call it dyed.) Anyway, it starts with that treatment, and then they apply the colour that is on the box.

If, for example, you are looking at a box of colour like 8g warm medium blonde, and you have light brown hair, that box will not give you 8g warm blonde! Why? Because that 8g on the box was done on a head of hair that was bleached, not on light brown hair! If you want that 8g warm medium blonde colour, then what do you think you need? Right: You have to go lighter, like a 10g or even higher. That 8g will probably give you just one shade of lift, and maybe not even that.

So in this case, if you are medium brown and want to go to medium blonde or a light blonde, I would first go to your salon and find out from your hairdresser what would be the right colour for you. Be honest, if you can't afford him or her every month, then say so. Your hairdresser will advise you as to what number to buy, and yes, all colour has a number attached to it, especially the ones you buy in the supermarket or chemist's.

Obviously, if you are already having your hair coloured at a salon, then you don't even need to read this chapter. But you never know, there might be something here that could save you a few bucks. Basically, though, I'm speaking to those who do their own colour at home. Read on for a few more colour tips.

GETTING THE GRAYoUT

When you're covering gray, remember that it's harder to cover gray in coarse, thick hair than in medium to fine hair. When choosing a colour to cover gray, a neutral colour—and it will say "neutral"—will cover gray best. Not ash or gold or red. (Unless your hair is golden blonde or honey red; then you'd use the colour on the box.) Neutral neutral neutral! You do want to cover that gray, don't you?

«Gray-BUSTERS,
— *really work.*» —

A GOOD RULE OF THUMB is that, because the hair colour on the box is applied to bleached hair, and your gray hair is white and/or silver, then the colour you choose from the box will be pretty true. For example, again using medium brown as a reference point: If your hair is medium brown with 50 percent gray, you can be safe in choosing the medium-brown colour that is on the box. Do not try to change or lighten your colour with this formula. This only applies to covering gray.

The only problem I can see is that some gray hairs are really colour-resistant and may take a longer processing time. So, please please please, follow the directions. If it says to leave the colour on the roots for twenty minutes and then comb through, by all means DO IT!

KEEP UP WITH TOUCHUPS
Be sure you don't wait too long to do your touchups. The longer you wait, the longer your roots become, and the more difficult it is to achieve a uniform colour from root to end.

THE COLOUR SCALE

I know I've been talking about colour levels, and you may be a little confused. But it's really pretty simple: Black is 1, blonde is 12, and everything else is in between. (Just kidding.) It normally goes like this:

12	LIGHTEST BLONDE		6	MEDIUM RED
11	VERY LIGHT BLONDE		5	DARK RED
10	LIGHT BLONDE		4	LIGHT BROWN
9	MEDIUM BLONDE		3	MEDIUM BROWN
8	DARK BLONDE		2	DARK BROWN
7	LIGHT RED		1	BLACK

«ADDING colour CAN REALLY, *plump up* YOUR HAIR.»

YOUR PERFECT colour

If you asked me what colour will work best for you, I'd have to tell you that this is one of those areas that require a one-on-one, face-to-face consultation. Choosing the perfect colour isn't as easy as it looks.

I remember years ago when the whole season/colour thing was in fashion. From the colour of your skin, eyes, and so on, some well-trained, well-intentioned person would tell you if you were a spring, summer, fall, or winter. Whether there's any truth in this approach is not something that I would dare to go into here. But as I said earlier in this chapter, I believe corrective colour or a drastic change in colour should be done by a pro.

Hopefully, one day I can meet you, and we can talk about your colour in person. There are a few other things we can discuss here, though: two products that you'll really love.

Streaking Kits

The first product I want to talk about is those streaking kits that you see on the shelves. Those products really do work.

The truth is, I did all those streaking commercials for Clairol a few years ago, remember the ones with the girls having a streaking party. I never paid much attention to the party concept because I was too busy making sure my twenty clients were all happy. Yeah. You cannot believe how many people show up for some of these things, and everyone, I mean everyone, has an opinion. It's really nuts, and that's the truth. I'm not mad at anyone; I love doing hair commercials because they're so challenging. But those advertising agencies hire *way* too many people, and very few, if any, know anything about hair!

STREAK IT SLOWLY

With streaking products, timing is important. Follow directions, and keep your hair saturated. You don't want to take it off too soon.

Anyway, I did those commercials, and those kits do work. The trick is, you have to read all the instructions. Read read read, and then read them again. They have it all written out for you, really they do, they have done a great job of it. So pay attention to the details when you decide to give your hair a little oomph!

Stains

The other products for colour are the semipermanent ones that stain your hair. Now, I have used these many times in the past, mostly to match hair extensions for a client. They are great for this, but for you, I think that they're great in between colourings, like for touch-ups. The semipermanent glosses are also great for exact colour matches.

Let's say you are two weeks into your colour and you are starting to see roots. That nasty regrowth is coming back, and you are busy, but you really need to do something because you have something important to do, or you just don't want to look at those roots (or let anyone else look at them).

No worries. Just find the semipermanent colour that's the same as the colour you are using. (They are matched numerically the same way as permanent colour.) This product comes in a mousse, so it's really easy to apply.

Semipermanent stains last anywhere from two to six weeks, depending on the type of hair you use it on. On resistant gray hair, it usually lasts in the two-week range.

But on porous, damaged hair, like all other hair products, it will stain your hair and might never come out!

The good news is, you need to buy these types of products at the beauty supply store, and usually, I said *usually*, they have someone on staff that knows what they are talking about. If you're in doubt about colour or type, ask.

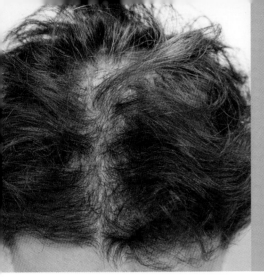

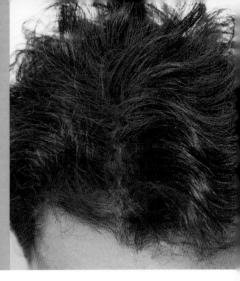

COLOURED DRY SHAMPOO

Look at these photos of just one example of how to use coloured dry shampoo. I mentioned how great of a product it was on page 62, but I think these photos speak for themselves!

COOKING UP GREAT colour

BOTTOMS UP

Ever wonder why they ask you start at the back of your head when you apply colour? It's because heat rises, so the nape of your neck takes longer to process. When you get to the top, your head is hotter and therefore, you process colour more quickly there. Now, that's not brain surgery, it's just the truth.

I need to say something here because it really applies to any chemical treatment for you hair. And this is it: Though I agree that you can most definitely use the hair colour you buy at the chemist's or supermarket, I think that you'll have the most success with home colouring if you are graying or if you're just SLIGHTLY changing your colour. (By that I mean, adding the same colour as your existing colour to add richness or going darker.) Anything that requires more calls for a pro. You know what I'm talking about. If you doubt anything that I'm saying, go to a pro and see the difference for yourself.

Let me say something else about colour: There is no magic to hair colour. It's like baking a cake. You have a recipe, and you need to follow that recipe. The instructions on the back of colour boxes are there for a reason! Any great colourists will follow the same recipe over and over again. If it's not broke, right?!

You see what I'm saying. I am certain that there will be colourists out there who will disagree with me, but hey, that's their choice. If you want beautiful colour, follow the recipe!

YOU DESERVE IT

I will tell you one last thing that may seem contradictory after giving you all these tips about colouring your own hair. I really think that you deserve to go to the salon. Seriously. It is a place of refuge in this weary, sometimes overcrowded world we live in. I have been healed and have healed others. So give yourself a break, go to a salon, and treat yourself.

« WHEN YOU DON'T HAVE THE MONEY for a salon, — *find a beauty school* — TO DO YOUR COLOUR. »

ROBERT STYLES
THE STARS

One of my clients has amazing Latin hair—it's this beautiful auburn. Well, to save her hair from constant colouring, because we were promoting her latest album at the time, I would use this semipermanent colour in between. It was perfect and covered the regrowth perfectly.

ROBERT STYLES
THE STARS

Do you remember those Old Navy commercials when they used all the actors from the '70s? Well, I was fortunate to have worked on most of them, and it was a thrill for me because I graduated in 1973 and those sitcom stars were part of my life.

Morgan Fairchild was in a few of those, and she is a doll. The director wanted her to have her hair highlighted, so he called me, and production set up an appointment at a very famous salon in Beverly Hills.

The woman who did Morgan's hair does a thing called belliage, which is a process of painting on colour or bleach like in those streaking commercials. Belliage is only good for short hair. It has a higher level of peroxide. And it's difficult to do and not overlap precoloured hair, which results in breakage.

So I, who know a thing or two about colour, asked her why. I really wanted Morgan's hair foil-highlighted because I believe that it's better; you cannot control colour when it's painted on randomly. Not to mention, when you paint on colour, it's impossible to protect the other hairs that have already been processed.

Then this stylist proceeds to tell me how old-fashioned foil highlighting is and that their salon only does belliage and it's state-of-the-art and blah blah blah! Nonsense, it's a marketing scam, plain and simple: You can fit more clients into your schedule if you're painting than if you were doing foils.

Hair colouring is an art form, yes, and this is not to say that there aren't some people who are better colourists than others. All I'm saying here is stick to the basics again. There is no shortcut when it comes to colour, yeah sure, it may work once, like the first time and even the second. But show me that belliage head of hair after even three applications versus a foil-highlighted head of hair after three applications, and I assure you that the belliage head will have way more breakage than the foiled one.

FAKE HAIR: Extensions and Wigs

chapter 7

FINE

VERINA

I used extensions to give Verina three different looks, as you'll see on the following pages. First, I applied one track to add volume, giving her a sweet but sexy look. Next, I added length for a lush, luxuriant style. And finally, I used a top piece along with the extensions to give Verina real siren appeal.

VERINA

Prepping the Hair for Track Extensions

1 Because Verina's hair is fine, I use little or no styling product on her hair. Instead, I just spritzed her hair with water to dampen it.

2 I parted her hair down the middle.

3 I sectioned off her hair by making a part on top on the head from in front of the crown to behind the ears.

4 I clipped the side sections up out of the way.

5 Starting in the front bang section, I used a large, round brush and blow dryer to smooth and straighten the hair.

Prepping the Back

1 I took down the first section, working from the bottom. I used large sections when blowing and smoothing with the round brush.

2 I turned the brush in the opposite direction at the roots.

3 I brought down the next section from the top, and continued until all the hair had been smoothed.

4 I used the flat iron to smooth the ends.

HAIR TEXTURE:
FINE

FIRST LOOK

One Single-Track Extension to Add Volume

[1] First, I needed to measure and cut the extension. As I combed and smoothed Verina's hair, I placed the extension on top of her hair to determine the length.

[2] I cut the length of the track a good inch to 2 inches (5 cm) below Verena's actual hair length. Professionals should block, cut, and style the track on a wig block. Don't cut the track on the client's head.

[3] Next, I texturized and slightly layered the ends of the track with a razor.

Applying a Track

[1] I sectioned the top of Verina's head with a semicircle parting under the crown to along the sides.

[2] Next, I backcombed the root area underneath the semicircle parting. (By backcombing, I mean take a fine-tooth comb 2 inches (5 cm) away from the scalp and push forward twice.)

[3] Then I applied the single track right under the parting, clipping it in place. I combed it in place to blend.

[4] I used a curling iron to smooth and blend Verena's natural hair with the extension track along the outside perimeter.

THE LAYERED LOOK

When you pin the track on the wig block, it is pinned straight across the block. But when the track is clipped onto the client's head, the contour of the person's head creates a shorter, layered effect on the sides.

HAIR TEXTURE:

FINE

Triple Tracks

Triple tracks are a fast, easy way to add a lot of volume behind the ears and around the back of the head. They can add a lot of length as well. This type of track can be as long as you like! A triple track is cut the same way a single track is cut, texturizing and slightly layering the ends. A triple track extension is usually placed a little lower than the single track, with the single track placed on top of and above it.

1 To section Verina's hair for the triple track extension, I made a semicircle parting that started behind the top of one ear and curved down around the back of the head to behind the top of the opposite ear.

2 I layered the track to blend with Verina's natural length.

3 I backcombed at the roots so the clips would have something to grab onto. I also sprayed a little hair spray.

4 Then I clipped the center clip into place first and worked to clip each side securely.

5 I placed the single track above the triple track so it lies on top of the triple track.

DON'T LENGTHEN LAYERS

If your hair is very layered, stay away from too much length when you choose extensions. Long extensions are more difficult to blend.

FINE

THIRD LOOK

Adding a Top Piece

[1] I textured Verina's fringe and length slightly with a razor to remove excess bulk.

[2] I styled the top piece on a wig block with a curling iron, creating soft waves.

The top piece can be lighter than the other tracks previously applied.

[3] Next, I created a middle part.

[4] To attach the top piece, I clipped it on in front, clipping at the hairline. Then I attached the sides.

[5] Then I used a little texturizing styling cream to blend.

[6] I used a curling iron to blend and curl the fringe and the rest of the top piece with the track below.

DRY SHAMPOO TO THE RESCUE

To cover root regrowth, you can spray on coloured dry shampoo. It also adds texture to the root area as well as absorbing oils.

fabulous
REVEЯSE

Let's keep the fun going. We all know you can dramatically change the appearance of your hair by using extensions. And I'm talking dramatically.

But this is one area where I will insist that you initially consult with your haircare professional. It is just not possible for you to use extensions unless you have them cut by your hairstylist. I am even doubtful that you can purchase them without having some knowledge of colour as well.

So taking it from the top, consult consult consult. It's not worth the money if you don't. Period. Even if the extensions are mine, and you buy them from me, I will insist that you go have them cut by your hairstylist.

I'm glad we've cleared that up. Let's move on to what extensions can do for you!

well as length to your hair. For example, you can use one track to give your hair some added volume, and then your second track to give it more length. You can also use these amazing tracks to add depth of colour or highlights. There are so many possibilities!

One of my secrets to getting great hair is to use the best hair extensions. I recommend Top Secret Haircessory. You can see their line of extensions at www.topsecrethair.com. Tell them I sent you.

STACIE

Here's how to do what I call a "reverse makeover"—adding length by adding one track of extensions.

STACIE

Reverse Makeover

1. Section off crown section.

2. Apply one track extension at occipital area.

3. Straighten top layer with flat iron to blend.

4. Use ¾-inch (19 cm) iron to create rounded ends.

5. Curl sides back and away from face as well as in opposite direction.

6. Use styling cream to separate curls.

Note: Because Stacie's hair is blonder and shorter on top, I matched the extension to her top colour.

Short Haircut and Style

When Stacie's not wearing her extensions, she still wants to look good. Here I gave her more glam by using texture cream to create movement and definition.

1. First, I gave Stacie a razored, choppy cut.

2. I blew her hair dry with little direction—no brushes, just air at the roots.

3. I used a styling cream for separation.

FINE

TERRI

Here's how to add length and change colour with my signature "reverse makeover."

With a top and back piece, it's a no-brainer!

HAIR TEXTURE:
FINE

TERRI

Reverse Makeover

[1] First, I blew out Terri's natural hair.

[2] I straightened her natural hair with a flat iron.

[3] I place the first track between the crown area and the occipital area. As you can see, it starts from one side and moves right around the back of the head to the other side.

[4] I textured and layered the ends of the hair track with a razor.

[5] I used Top Secret Hair (www.topsecrethair.com) extensions in a colour that was a blend of Terri's own colour.

[6] The top piece, also from Top Secret Hair, is clipped into place. I blended Terri's own fringe into the top piece.

MAKING THE CUT

Place the extension over your head and mark where it needs to be cut, perhaps by clipping off a little piece at the right length. Then remove the extension to cut it to length. If you don't have a wig head to place it on to make the cut, you can put the extension on the back of a sofa or soft chair.

« **I never** CUT
the extension
WHEN IT'S ON
MY GIRL'S HEAD. »

Elegant Variation

If Terri doesn't want to wear her extensions, it's easy to style her hair in this simple, elegant updo.

1. For this style, I backcombed Terri's whole head. Starting at the top, I worked my way down.

2. Next, I created fullness at the crown area.

3. The third step is to spray with hairspray.

4. I smoothed Terri's hair with a boar-bristle paddle brush, moving back and up from the nape to occipital height.

5. I gave Terri a ponytail, then took the ponytail and twisted it in a downward direction so her hair would make a twist.

6. Taking the end of the twist, I tucked it back underneath the hair at the bottom.

7. I secured the hair with bobby pins along the twist underneath so that you can see the bobby pins. The bobby pins hold the twist against the scalp securely.

8. I used hairpins to further secure the twist.

9. I added a hair ornament at the twistline to give the style additional sophistication while concealing the pins.

PERMA NENT EXtensions

There are also permanent extensions, which are applied pretty much strand by strand. Here's how it works: We take about ten of your own hairs at a time, then we either glue the extension hair on or use a polyurethane product to adhere the extension to your hair. There is also a method in which a metal clamp attaches the extension to your hair near the roots.

All three of these application techniques are really tough on your hair. But if you have strong hair, then go for it. Otherwise, if your hair is fine or medium fine and is vulnerable, then stay away from this type of attachment. Also, if you have thick, wavy hair, permanent extensions are probably not a good idea, because you'll have a hard time matching the extension to your own hair, given your hair's density.

There is also another way to apply permanent extensions, and that is to glue the track directly to your hair roots. (Be sure the glue's on your hair, not your scalp.) This is common among African-American women. African-American women have stronger hair in general. Their hair and scalp can handle the wear and tear of the glue-on hair extensions.

I used to use only glue-on extensions with my clients just because we didn't have the choices that we have today. It was a pain, because most of them wanted to take them out at night, and then I had to put them back in the morning. Not fun.

But if you're getting married, for example, and you want longer hair for the wedding, I think that the week of your wedding is a great time to do any of the permanent attachment-type extensions. There's no reason to wait until the last minute. Getting them done earlier in the week will make your wedding week that much more stress free.

ROBERT STYLES
THE STARS

You may have wondered if movie stars' and models' hair can really be as lush as it looks. Well, here's the truth: I use hair extensions with some of my clients on a day-to-day basis. Unfortunately, I can't tell you who I use them on. It wouldn't be nice, and furthermore, it would ruin the illusion that we work so hard to create for you. Most of the time, it's for the purpose of the shoot or to create an image, anyway, not a round-the-clock look.

Here's one example I can share with you. I was working with Hilary Swank, who has a ton of hair and never needs extensions. However, on a recent photo shoot, the photographer wanted Hilary to have a fringe. So, instead of cutting a fringe, I reached for a type of extension called a top piece from my friend Denise Russo, who designs and sells hair extensions (www.topsecrethair.com). The top piece is like a mini-wig, sort of like a toupee but smaller. It sits on the top of your head and can change your look in an instant, adding volume, colour, and depth. In our case that day, I used the top piece to create a fringe. I clipped it right on like any other hair extension, combed it down in front of Hil's face, and cut a fringe.

REAL FAKE HAIR
VS. FAKE FAKE HAIR

I absolutely have to tell you about the difference between using synthetic hair extensions as opposed to human hair. I am truly sorry for those of you who went out and spent your hard-earned money on synthetic hair extensions. This is not the same as a synthetic wig.

A wig is worn over your whole head, and your own hair is placed underneath the wig, so a synthetic wig can look natural. Hair extensions, on the other hand, are meant to be blended with your own hair. And believe me, synthetic extensions mixed into real hair is not a pretty sight, nor is it possible to blend them properly.

I have seen the same infomercials for synthetic hair extensions that you have, and I'm amazed that the count clicker just keeps going up and up. It's unbelievable how many woman buy these things.

Here is the truth: Synthetic hair is made out of man-made fiber. There are different types, but none of them match human hair. A natural hair extension is made one way and one way only, out of human hair. What you see is what you get.

DRAMA QUEEN

You can backcomb at the root of the top section on the track and work with your fingers to style and separate the curls for more volume and drama.

There is no way that your human hair can blend with the synthetic stuff, it just isn't gonna happen, period, end of story. Hate me, you manufacturers that make this stuff, sue me if you like, but you will never convince me that it works. It's amazing: Even on the commercial, you can see the difference! I can't believe it.

The only time a synthetic fiber can and should be used is on a wig.

These wigs are made to order, and I've seen some amazing ones. They usually fit great and need little if any cutting. They are easy to maintain, because they keep their shape no matter what. And they're easy to wash, because when they dry, they go right back to the wave pattern that they came with. Even the cut, after washing, usually requires just a little brushing.

Do I think that these wigs look natural? Well, no, but I have a trained eye. They usually have an unnatural shine that human hair just doesn't have.

Let's just say that synthetics are better as wigs than as extensions. Until I am convinced otherwise, stay away from synthetic extensions, but go for it with the synthetic wig.

I could spend another ten chapters on hair pieces and wigs, and who knows, maybe I'll do a book on that as well. But for the moment, we are keeping it basic and simple. And really, for today's styles, extensions are where it's at.

COLOUR ON TRACK

The colour of the extension track can be a shade darker than the natural hair that will be blended over it. (Check the colour of the shaft and ends of the natural hair for the true colour.) A darker track blends better than a lighter colour and looks more natural. I do like to use the darker colour underneath for more depth. However, this can be tricky, since most women have much lighter hair on the top of their heads. This is just a general rule. Many times, I do use lighter tracks to blend with the top colour.

«It's ALL about
— *proportion* AND *balance* —
WHEN IT COMES TO CHOOSING
THE LOOK
THAT'S RIGHT FOR YOU.»

Part III

STYLE SECRETS: From Good to GREAT Hair

HAIR CUTTING

THIS IS NOT A HAIR CUTTING GUIDE. I am not about to tell you how to cut hair. It's not possible. I can, however, give you some basic knowledge about haircutting that you will find interesting. And having this knowledge will definitely give you some insight to your own haircut.

THE BLUNT CUT

Let's start out with the infamous "blunt cut." First of all, a blunt cut is not a hairstyle. It's a technique. In the case of the blunt cut, the word "blunt" pertains to the hair itself. A blunt cut is done with shears, used as shears were originally designed to be used. If one hair was your finger, and you cut the tip off straight across with one motion of the shears, then it would be a blunt cut.

If the hair is cut at an angle, it would still be blunt, but we hairdressers would not consider that a blunt cut, because by cutting the hair at that angle the weight would shift. Today's hairstyles are more "sliced" than blunted, but blunt-cutting is still incorporated into the cut.

« **Remember** — *the term 'blunt'* — refers to technique, NOT STYLE. »

Now, not to confuse you too much, blunt cuts are most commonly referred to as bobs and/or what you would consider to be one-length hair. A blunt cut is great for bobs because it gives weight to the end of the hair. But remember that the term refers to a technique, not a style. You can layer your whole head and still be using the "blunt" haircutting technique. See what I mean?

DON'T FORGET TO TRIM

Whenever I'm trimming someone's hair to just take off the split ends, I always use the blunt technique. That reminds me: I recommend that you have your hair trimmed at least once every two months, even when—no, especially when—you are trying to grow your hair.

Did you ever get to that point when you are trying to grow out your hair and it seems to not grow any longer? Guess what, unless you trim, it will never get past that length. Yes, it's true that some women's hair just doesn't grow that long. But most people can have long hair with good hair care and frequent trims.

When I say "trim," I mean it literally: Take those ends off. Your ends have a mind of their own and can easily split and break, even when you're asleep. Yep, when you are sleeping. The tossing and turning on the pillow can cause friction and the ends tangle, and voilà, broken hairs. And of course they can split when you're awake, too! So make a standing appointment to have them trimmed regularly.

«You need TO HAVE YOUR HAIR TRIMMED
— *at least once every two months* —
ESPECIALLY WHEN YOU'RE TRYING
TO GROW YOUR HAIR.»

ALEXANDRA

This is a complete makeover.

I took Alexandra's hair from straight to great, using shears for the cut and then razoring the ends slightly for texture. Don't try this at home!

HAIR TEXTURE:
MEDIUM

ALEXANDRA

Haircut Makeover

[1] I cut about 12 inches (30 cm) off of Alexandra's hair, creating a graduated textured bob.

[2] Next, I applied texture cream to finish Alexandra's style.

[3] After finishing the cut, I blew Alexandra's hair dry without using any type of product on it. I blew the hair under to style it.

[4] Finally, I used a wide-toothed brush for extra direction on the ends.

« HERE'S SOME MATH
— *we can all remember:* —
A GREAT CUT + GREAT STYLE
= GREAT HAIR. »

«IT'S **all** — *in the* CUT!» —

THICK
curly

Jean

What if you'd like a bob but your hair is curly? I gave Jean a haircut makeover with a graduated textured bob on curly hair.

THICK
curly

Jean

Haircut Makeover

1. I straightened Jean's curly hair with a blow dryer.

2. With a thinning shear, I chopped into the outer layer. I removed length and bulk at the same time.

The Style

1. I sectioned off Jean's hair so I would be able to work in manageable areas on her head.

2. Using a large, round brush, I blew-dry to straighten Jean's hair to create smooth waves.

Because her hair is wavy, I started on the front sides to smooth before her hair dried.

3. I alternated the direction of the round brush from section to section, directing the hair from right to left, so that the style didn't turn out too perfect and "done" looking. By using this technique to take advantage of Jean's curly hair, her own natural curl took over the ends!

4. Finally, I blew the back in a downward direction.

THE RIGHT STUFF

To style Jean's thick, curly hair, I used smoothing cream with a bit of Texture Twist. Not too heavy, not too light. Just the perfect amount!

«Wet CUTS
— on curly hair —
SHRINK IN LENGTH ONCE
THE HAIR IS DRIED.»

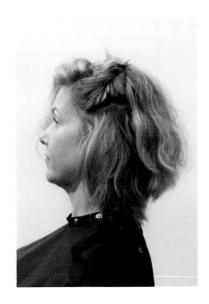

MAKING
THE cUT

Razors and shears are the tools of the haircutting trade. The next time your stylist cuts your hair, sit back and watch the show. Good stylists are artists. A great stylist can do scissor cutting in ways that you never thought possible.

Thinning shears are the scissors with a blade on one side and a metal comb on the other. Used primarily by barbers, they were originally intended to taper the hair for a man's haircut. (You know when you can see the marks on your husband's hair after his hair has been cut? Well, this can be avoided by using thinning shears.) When they're used properly, they can fine-tune a choppy cut.

It's awesome how some hairstylists can handle a pair of shears, flying through the hair like Edward Scissorhands. But those thinning shears can do serious damage if in the wrong hands.

The truth is, there are so many ways to use all of these tools. It still amazes me when I see hairdressers that use them as if they were conducting an orchestra. It's a beautiful thing to watch.

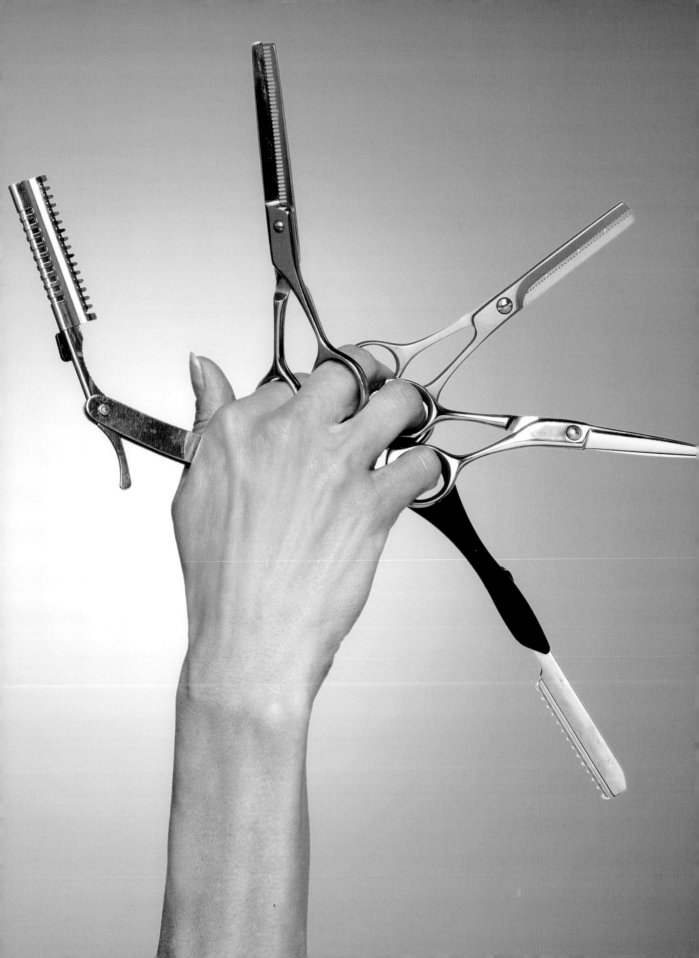

CUTTING DRY Hair

Dry cutting is my preferred method of cutting hair. I blow the hair dry and straighten it and then cut. It is by far the best way to see how the hair will fall. Even the curliest heads can be cut this way, and you will be amazed how your hair will maintain a style if cut dry. I mean really, how many times have you had your haircut the standard way—while it's wet— only to watch your hairstylist then cut more and more and more after it's dry? Right?

This method was made popular years ago by a genius hairdresser, by the name of John Sahag. John was a great man, a great hair- dresser and an innovator. He developed this special way of cutting, and everyone in his very successful salon in New York City cuts the exact same way; it is foolproof. I know, because I worked there on one of my stays in the city.

At one point I decided to move back to the United States and took an apartment in New York City.

I went to see John, thinking that I might get back into salon work. And although I freelanced, and wanted to continue, John saw that the future for freelance hairdressers was heading in the direction of combining your salon work with studio work. So he accepted me and I started in his salon, at first as an observer to learn his technique, and then eventually to start cutting.

I'm talking about this chapter in my life for two reasons: one, to pay homage to a great man who maintained the highest standards in the industry, and two, to validate my experience. You see, John was one of the very few who did studio work as well as main- taining a salon clientele. His client list was a "who's who" in the celebrity and fashion world. His was the career to emulate.

As I was only freelance at the time, it was an honour to be accepted by John, and had I stayed, I would have been the only other hair- dresser on his staff that did both studio and salon work. But my life took another direction. I decided to move back to Europe and ended up in a small seaport in the south of France called Cassis. It's a long story, but suffice it to say, the year 1991 was a pivotal year for me, and John Sahag was a part of that. Thank you, my friend.

TRIMMING YOUR FRINGE

There are no shortcuts and very few tips I can give you about cutting hair. The only tip I'm comfortable giving you is for trimming your fringe. This technique will give you beautifully rounded fringe.

Here's what to do: After your fringe has been cut, separate it into three sections. Comb each section forward, starting with the sides and then doing the middle section. Grab the hair in each section together as if you were pinching it. Bring the pinched section to the top of the bridge of your nose and then cut, facing the shears or scissors horizontally. A good rule of thumb is to cut between your brow and your eyelashes—somewhere in the middle of the two. As you grab your hair from left to right and vice versa, the distance from the side to the middle, when you've finished cutting, is what gives you the rounded effect.

To achieve a more piecey effect, after cutting, comb your fringe into place and using the scissors vertically, make little notches across your fringe. Just notch the tips, though.

LARISA

I gave Larisa a haircut to shape her style. In her case, the upswept fringe is the key to the whole look.

MEDIUM

LARISA

The Style

[1] Once I'd given Larisa her cut, it was time to create her new style. I used a heat protector that has a setting element.

[2] I used a small, round brush to blow hair all the way back away from Larisa's face.

[3] I started at the fringe area, away from the face.

[4] Next, I blew the rest of the style, lifting at the root.

[5] I brushed the style out with a boar-bristle paddle brush.

[6] I used spray gel and texture cream to keep Larisa's new look in place.

«WHETHER short OR long, — *back* AND *away* — IS BEST!»

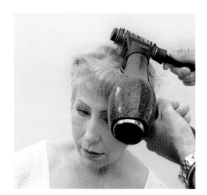

SHOW YOUR FACE

At a certain age, I believe that a woman's hair looks best away from her face. That's because hair worn down on the face after a certain age creates shadows, and you know that's not flattering. Whether short or long, back and away is best! Wearing your hair off your face gives the illusion of lifting, making you look younger and more radiant. If you don't like your forehead and insist on covering it, at least move the direction of your hair or fringe away from your face.

MEDIUM
curly

Annette

Annette wanted to keep

her length, so all I did was modernize

her look. I gave her a cut that framed her

face and texturized the ends of her hair.

It's amazing what a little blow-drying and

a flat iron, along with the right cut, can do!

HAIR TEXTURE & TYPE:

MEDIUM
curly

Annette

Haircut Makeover

[1] To prep Annette's hair for the cut, I applied a quarter-size dab of leave-in conditioner cream to the wet hair.

[2] I sectioned off her hair into two big sections, with a part from the crown to behind the ears.

[3] Starting from the back, I took down a section of hair and pinned the remainder up. Then I blew the small section smooth and dry with a large, round brush.

[4] I continued up the head, bringing each small section down at a time and drying with the brush and dryer.

[5] I spritzed on an anti-frizz oil/ serum on each section and used a flat iron to smooth the hair one section at a time.

[6] To cut Annette's hair, I used a combination of thinning shears and regular shears. I used the regular shears to create the outline.

[7] Then I used the thinning shears to remove bulk and length, mostly on the ends.

[8] Next, I created a little height at the crown by lifting the roots with a comb and using a blow dryer at the roots.

[9] I allowed the root area to cool as I lifted the hair with the comb to set the root lift.

«Never UNDERESTIMATE
the power of thinning
TO SHAPE A LOOK!»

RAZOR CUTS

Razor cuts should only be done by someone who knows what they are doing.

I don't recommend trying this at home. The basic idea with a razor cut is to remove bulk from your hair while at the same time keeping your length.

Razor cutting was used a lot during the '50s and '60s. It was a great way to slice the hair to achieve the length on top so you could then tease the heck out of it. The beautician (the term of the day; I still like it) would cut your hair close to the neck and short around the sides, and leave the hair on top at least 6 to 12 inches (15 to 30 cm) long. If your hair was thick, they would take a razor and remove the bulk, leaving just enough to give a good base. Then the long part was teased and backcombed into these amazing, bulletproof shapes.

It is on this classic style that I learned my craft. Yes, it's true. Here's the story. This was the time when women would get their hair washed and set on Saturday, then get a comb-out on Wednesday or Thursday. Now, every other night, my mom and aunts Bea Bea and Marie would sit around our kitchen table, gabbin' away, while we kids would run in and out of the house, making them nuts. I have seven siblings, so all of us and our friends created quite a scene.

WHEN NOT TO USE A RAZOR CUT

It's not a good idea to razor curly and/or coarse hair. The reason curly hair is curly is because of its cuticle layer (remember the shingles on the roof?). Well, with curly hair, the cuticle layer is open, pretty much all over the place really. That's why you rarely see shiny curly hair and why curly hair has a tendency to be dry. If you start to razor the curly hair, it just slices it up all over the place. So blunt-cut it; your hair will love you for it.

RAZOR CUTS DONE RIGHT

I recommend that if you do have your hair razor cut, then spread out the razor cuts over time. In other words, it's not a good idea to get a razor cut over and over again. That's because using a razor has a tendency to really thin out your hair, so be careful to not overdo it. I would only have it cut with the razor every third haircut.

Shears cutting as if the shears were a razor, slicing the hair or sliding the blades, is pretty much the same idea as a razor cut, but with more precision. This technique can have the same thinning effect as razor cutting, but since it's much more controllable, it enables your stylist to do less thinning.

Well, during one of those kitchen-table Rocco sisters' conferences, I started to play with my mom's petal curls. Her hair was already a mess, so I don't think she cared, in fact, I'm sure she really didn't even know I was touching her hair. (Please, you could grow stuff in there!) Anyway, I realized that I could return that petal curl back into its original shape, and so I did the rest of my mom's hair, and my aunts', too.

After that, on any Thursday night at the Vetica house, you could find me recombing my mom's and aunts' hair. I wasn't permitted to tell anyone, 'cause boys didn't do those things where I came from, so I kept my secret for a while. Forget about a closeted homosexual, I was a closeted beautician. It was a few years later that I flew out of both closets, but that's another book!

I learned real hairdressing from those days. Shapes and forms are what it's all about, and when I cut hair, I still do it the same way that I did then. I learned originally by osmosis. Then I went to beauty school.

VERY FINE

DANIELLE

I gave Danielle a layered makeover cut. Now her hairstyle matches her personality. Once again, it's all about the cut!

DANIELLE

Haircut Makeover

[1] I actually pulled Danny's hair to the crown for the cut, as you can see in the photos. It gave her a long shag look.

[2] As she already had a fringe, I took a razor and sliced into it to frame her face.

[3] I blew Danny's hair dry upside down and back and forth. No brush, no comb, no product. Perfect for Danielle's fine-textured hair!

[4] I finished with a little hair spray.

«I USE
— *little* OR *no product* —
IN FINE HAIR LIKE DANIELLE'S.»

MEDIUM
with a slight wave

Sandy

I wanted to give Sandy

more than a makeover cut. I added

a special "instant face-lift" hair trick.

Together with her updated style, it really

takes the years off, making her even

more beautiful.

MEDIUM
with a slight wave

Sandy

Haircut Makeover

1 I began by blowing Sandy's hair straight with a blow dryer.

2 As Sandy wanted to keep her length, I chopped into her hair with shears to soften the edges and remove length.

3 Of course, I gave her a fringe so she could wear it down or swept back to suit her mood and style.

The Style

1 For Sandy's beautiful wind-swept look, I blew her hair straight with a large, round brush and blow dryer.

2 I took sections starting in the front on the sides and curled them with a 1-inch (2.5 cm) curling iron in the middle of the hair shaft to create loose waves.

3 I spiraled the hair around the iron, moving away from Sandy's face.

4 I continued curling the whole head in the midshaft area.

5 I used a little bit of texture cream to finish the look. I applied about a dime-sized amount in my palm, then rubbed my palms together. I flipped Sandy's head over and started by applying texture cream to the layers underneath, working it into the waves of the hair.

INSTANT FACE- AND NECK-LIFTS

You can create a micro-mini-braid as I did for Sandy and position it above or below the eyebrow, depending on the individual. The same technique can be used at the nape for a mini neck-lift.

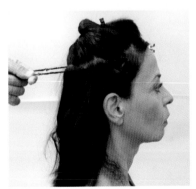

Fast Face-lift Trick

[1] I sectioned off the crown of the head and secured the hair in a clip.

[2] I created a micro-mini-braid on either side just above eyebrow height and a little in from the hairline, moving from the outer corner of the eye into the hairline diagonally.

[3] I secured the braids with tiny elastic bands. You can create an eyebrow lift at this level. If you create the braids back and in from the cheekbone area, you will get another face-lift effect. You can also experiment with micro-mini-braids to pull the skin taut under the jawline. It's cheaper than a face-lift and yet very effective.

[4] I used a micro elastic band to tie the two braids together just under the crown in the back of the head.

HAIR
STYLING
9
chapter

IT'S all YOU
ABOUT

As I travel around the world, I see women from every culture and
of every ethnic origin. But I never, ever look at someone and think,
"What would I do if she was sitting in my chair?"

When I worked in the salon, I styled women because they came
to me for my expertise, but I worked with them, not on them.
Today I do the same thing. When a woman is sitting in my chair,
I don't try to change her. All I want to do is polish the diamond,
as it were.

I think it's fantastic when I see a woman who still has perfect hair
that was teased and set. I love the Barbie hair, the Roaring Twenties
bob, the Farrah mane, Mohawks, pink hair, bleached blonde, anything that says, "Hey world, this is me and this is who I am!"

So I am not going to tell you how you should wear your hair in this
chapter. It just doesn't seem right. It's not who I am. I will, however,
share my style ideas with you and show you how I do what I do. You
can take it from there!

STRAIGHT

In this chapter, I will give you a blow-by-blow (pardon the French) on how to achieve the looks that you desire. I will take eleven women and style each of them several different ways. First, I'll do an initial style. The second and third (and maybe fourth) styles will be inspirational variations.

I'll provide corresponding how-to directions for each style, including specifics like what products I used and the appropriate curling iron and brush. When I use bobby pins and/or elastic bands, I'll show you those as well and give you a step-by-step guide. Of course, I'll tell you each model's hair texture so you can see how it compares to your own. I will also take the shape of each model's face into account, as well as her lifestyle.

curly

FACE shape,
HAIR, AND BEAUTY

Since we're on the subject, let's talk about face shape. As I was preparing myself to write this book, I was a little doubtful about this subject. I never really thought about women's faces in that way: whether your face is round, square, oval, heart-shaped, or pear-shaped. I learned about these face shapes from my friend Robert Jones's makeup book, *Makeup Makeovers*.

I had to think about this for a while. That's because I guess I naturally look at a woman's face shape as I'm cutting and styling her hair, without consciously putting that shape into a category. As I said early on, it's all about proportion and balance when you do hair. Haircutting is this way and so is styling. So whether you are choosing a new look or just want to change the look you have for an evening, it's all about proportion. And proportion is about more than just the shape of your face.

That's because, in hairstyling, we are dealing with the whole head, not just face shape. So maybe you have a perfect oval-shaped face, but you have a small head. Then I would need to add more layers around the region at the top of your head so it will give you more volume. So there is a little more to think about. Naturally, if you have a long face, you want to stay away from hair that is too long, and you would want to add layers to offset the length of your face.

But there's a bigger question, too: What are we judging beauty by? Oval, pear, square, round, or heart-shaped, does it really matter when we're talking about hair? Yes, I know it does. But there is a fine line to what this definition of perfect beauty really is. That is why I believe that it's all about proportion and balance when it comes to choosing the look that's right for you.

FINE
DENSE
STRAIGHT

JESSICA

If you have fine hair like Jessica's, you may have given up on styling altogether. But fear not, great hair is just a curling iron away!

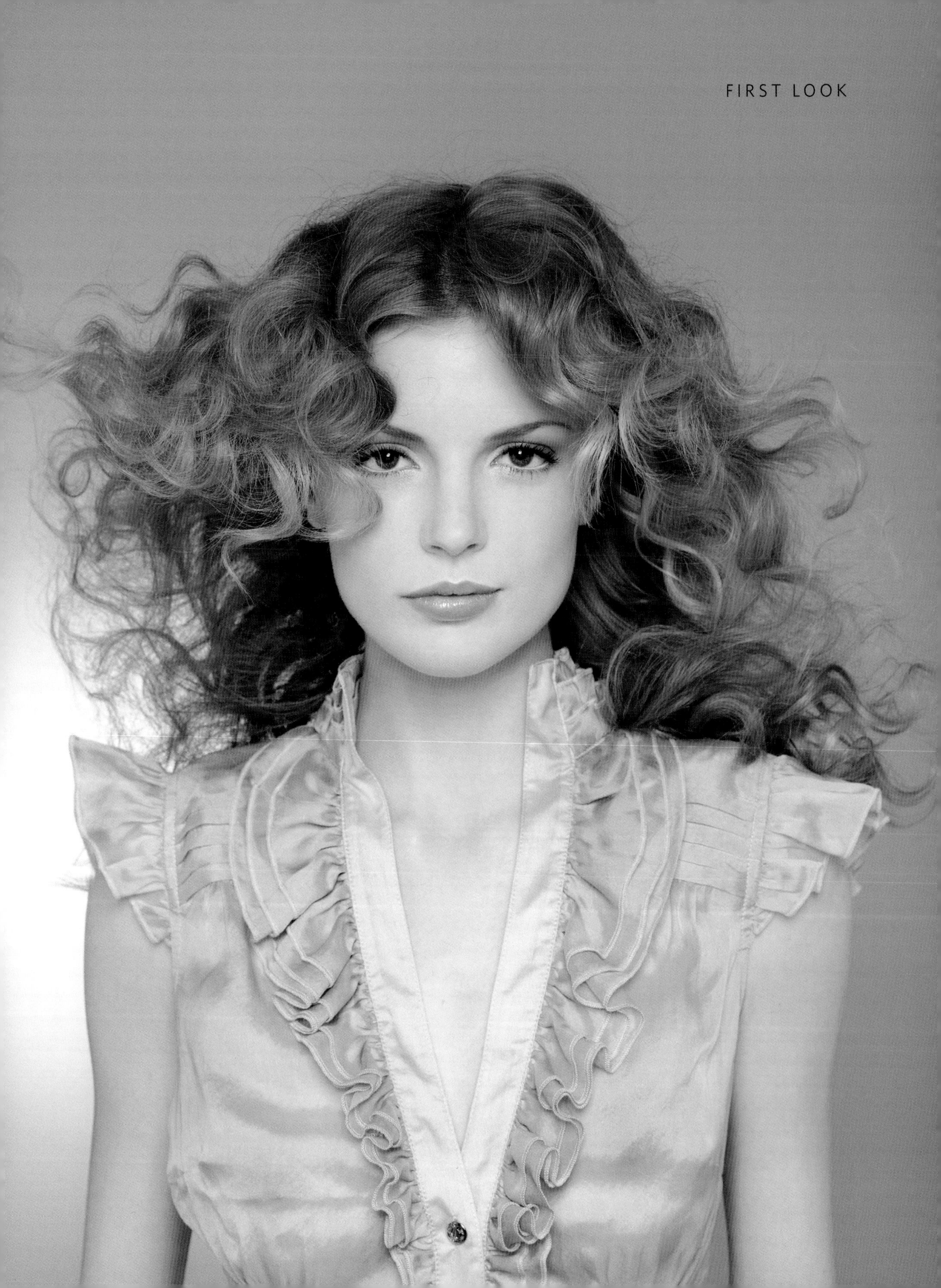

FINE
DENSE
STRAIGHT

FIRST LOOK

In this look, I gave Jessica a lot of fullness with romantic flyaway curls. She looks like she just stepped out of a romance novel!

1. Section the hair into big sections. Part it down middle; from the crown to behind the ears.

2. Create upper and lower sections on the side with a horizontal parting.

3. Take small 1 x 1-inch (2.5 x 2.5 cm) horizontal partings and wind each section around a curling iron with a ¼-inch (6 mm) barrel in a downward motion along the back, the sides, and finally the top.

4. After the curls cool, use a boar-bristle paddle styling brush to brush through the curls to break them up into a wave pattern.

5. Use a wide-tooth comb to back-comb in big sections.

6. Smooth hair into loose, curly waves.

7. Use a light mist of hair spray to finish.

SPIRALING HAIR

If you are right-handed, when spiraling hair on the left side of your head onto the curling iron, you need to approach the curling process from above the head.

*Arrow indicates curling iron direction.

HAIR TEXTURE & TYPE:
FINE
DENSE
STRAIGHT

SECOND LOOK

For this look, I kept the fullness around Jessica's face with lush curls, but pulled her hair back and pinned it in a sophisticated knot at the back. The result is a faux, wavy bob that combines romance and sophistication.

1 Starting with the same set as in the first look, brush through the hair with a boar-bristle paddle brush to loosen waves.

2 Using your hands only, comb through the hair with your fingers to create a low ponytail. Secure low ponytail with a covered band.

3 Gather, roll, and tuck the length of the ponytail under at the nape, and pin to hold it in place. It should look like a faux, wavy bob.

4 Finish by making loose waves with your fingers and a little hair spray. Frame the face with loose waves.

CREATE DIFFERENT CURLS

Here are two techniques you can use to create different curls using a curling iron:

1 If you wind the hair on the iron as you would on a curler—from the ends up to the roots—the curl pattern of the section will be tighter on the ends and gradually get larger as you wind the hair around the iron.

2 If you spiral the hair along the length of the barrel of the iron, the result will be a more uniform curl/wave pattern.

«Hairspray
— *is your friend here.* —
SPRITZ at the ROOTS
AFTER EACH SECTION IS TEASED.»

THIRD LOOK

Elegance is the word for this style. I backcombed the hair to give it height and fullness, contrasting it with the glossy smoothness of the hair in front of the headband. If you've always fantasized about looking like a princess, try this classic look.

1 Starting with the same set as in the first look, brush waves out with a boar-bristle paddle brush.

2 Use a blow dryer and styling brush to smooth and loosen the wave pattern a little.

3 Use a large comb to back-comb 2-inch (5 cm) sections, starting with the top front section and moving to the back of the head. Make sure to start your backcombing at the roots of each section.

4 Backcomb the side sections up towards the top of the head.

5 Place a headband over the head, then draw it back toward the crown to the correct positioning for a headband. You should have a lot of height and fullness at the crown.

6 Gather and twist the ends of the hair, turning them under, and pin them above the nape.

7 Use fingers and spray to create a full, rounded, romantic shape that is accented by the headband.

8 Finish by pinning a silk flower in place behind the right ear at the base of the headband on that side as an accent.

RESCUING OVER-
CURLED HAIR

If you think you have curled
too much, use a blow dryer
randomly to loosen.

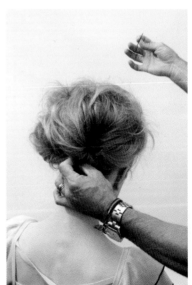

HAIR TEXTURE & TYPE:

THICK
COURSE
curly

Eileen

If your hair is thick and curly like Eileen's, you already know its challenges. You also know that pretty much all other women want hair just like yours!

HAIR TEXTURE & TYPE:

THICK
COURSE
curly

FIRST LOOK

Give your hair a touch of glam by turning those curls from wild to wow! with the techniques I used for this look.

We are just touching up Eileen's already-dried curls. And this is how we did it:

1 Section off the hair, starting from the bottom/back of the head.

2 Apply leave-in cream conditioner on each section.

3 Comb through the ends only.

4 Using ½-inch (13 mm) curling iron, wind each section around the shaft of the iron to the ends in a spiral, randomly curling some forward and some backward.

5 Spray liquid leave-in conditioner on the shaft of the hair to the ends. Also apply leave-in cream conditioner and silicone mixed together in your palm, used on shaft to ends.

6 Use two different-size curling irons, ½- and ¾-inch (13 and 19 mm) irons, to keep the curls from being too uniform.

7 Split back into three sections, one on each side and one section on the top. (You should not comb through the sections, but rather work through each section with your fingers.)

8 Use a little silicone on the finished curls to smooth them.

9 For the top, curl sections back away from the face.

10 Heat strands in front around the face at the hairline to smooth away from the face. Use silicone to finish waves—toss hair over and work product from nape to ends.

*Arrows indicate curling iron direction.

HAIR TEXTURE:

THICK

COURSE

curly

SECOND LOOK

I straightened Eileen's hair to give her an entirely new look. She's instantly transformed from footloose and fun-loving to cool and collected. This transformation is easier than it looks: All you need is a flat iron and a lot of leave-in conditioner and silicone to smooth those curly tresses.

1 Section off the back. Comb through curls and flat-iron one section at a time, making ¼- to ½-inch (0.6 to 1.25 cm) sections. Apply silicone as needed.

2 Bring each horizontal section down at a time until you work your way up the back of the head and the sides, continuing until you reach the part line on top of the head.

HAIR TEXTURE & TYPE:

THICK
COURSE
curly

THIRD LOOK

Eileen's first look is wild, carefree, romantic; her second look is sleek and sophisticated. For the third look, I combined both effects to create a sophisticated style that still has a hint of wildness. The effect is hot, foxy, but still in control—the best of both worlds!

[1] Using a 1¼-inch (32 mm) barrel curling iron, start with the frame of the face. Take big sections and curl them away from the face from mid-shaft to ends.

[2] Separate your hair from your crown to your neck and pull your hair forward.

[3] Curl using the same direction as you did in the front.

AVOID THE ALCOHOL!

If you have a thick, coarse, curly mane like Eileen's, you can use most products. But stay away from alcohol-based products like hair spray!

*Arrow indicates curling iron direction.

THICK
wavy

Rosemary

Rosemary's thick, wavy hair inspired me to recreate some of the classic Hollywood looks from the Golden Age of movie glamour, with a modern twist!

HAIR TEXTURE & TYPE:
THICK
wavy

FIRST LOOK

Check out that deep wave in Rosemary's first look—timeless '40s star glam.

1. First, create a deep side part.

2. Spray the heavy side of the parted hair with heat protector setting lotion spray. Fairly moisten the hair with the spray, but don't totally saturate it.

3. Use teeth of comb against the scalp to create the first wave curve, moving away from the forehead. Create a ridge.

4. Secure with a finger wave clamp to hold the ridge in place.

5. Hold the first wave in place as you drag the comb underneath it in the opposite direction to create the "S" wave pattern.

6. Secure with a finger wave clamp.

7. Create a horizontal parting along the occipital line of the head from where the wave in the front ends, moving around the back of the head.

8. Take vertical sections from the top half and curl with a curling iron, moving the curl toward the face on the heavy side.

9. Continue taking vertical sections of hair as you make your way around the back of the head, completing the top half first.

10. Then start on the bottom half, again taking vertical sections.

11. Curl the sections, moving in the opposite direction to the top half (away from the face on the opposite side). Continue moving all the way around the head to the other side.

12 Spray hair spray on the set when it's completed.

13 Remove the finger wave clamps, leaving the large silver clips to hold the waves in place.

14 Brush out the set with a boar-bristle paddle brush. Backcomb slightly, and use your fingers and comb to finish, creating waves that move into wavy curls at the bottom. Again, use hair spray.

«A DEEP
— side part —
ADDS DRAMA to
THE FACE.»

THICK
wavy

SECOND LOOK

Turning the heat up a notch, for the second look, I've taken Rosemary from '40s starlet to Marilyn Monroe.

1. Create a deep side part as for the first look.

2. Curl under the outside perimeter with a ½-inch (13 mm) curling iron, curling section by section.

3. In the front, the sections should move along the perimeter of the hairline diagonally (perpendicular to the hairline).

4. Secure with small silver pins.

5. To create the style, start by removing the pins. Pull the hair with your fingers.

6. Backcomb slightly with a large-tooth comb.

7. Wind and curl sections with your fingers and pin into place with bobby pins along the perimeter to create a Marilyn Monroe look.

SAVED BY SETTING LOTION

Today, I don't have the luxury of setting a woman's hair wet and then placing her under a hooded dryer like they did years ago. All these looks were achieved on dry hair using spray setting lotion. The setting lotion moistens the hair, making it easier to manipulate it, and it also protects hair from the heat.

THIRD LOOK

Think "Marlene Dietrich on the Beach" for the glam style seen above. This is casual swept-back elegance.

This is the same set as the second look, all I did was brush out the top and pull it into a pony.

HAIR TEXTURE & TYPE:

THICK
wavy

FOURTH LOOK

For a more contemporary, informal look, I backcombed Rosemary's hair, then pulled it back into a smooth chignon, giving her swirling fringe and some height at the crown. This look still gives Rosemary plenty of glam while giving her a kittenish appeal.

1. Follow steps from First Look.

2. Brush out set.

3. Lightly backcomb the whole head section by section.

4. Use a boar-bristle paddle brush to smooth backcombed hair to the nape of the neck. Make sure to leave some height at the crown and top area!

5. Use a covered band to create a low ponytail.

6. Wrap hair into a small bun at the nape and pin into place.

7. Smooth the front section into place to create a loose fringe sweep.

MEDIUM
STRAIGHT

ANNE

Anne has the perfect combo of medium texture with medium density. Although straight, her hair holds whatever curl I put in. She has hair with memory!

HAIR TEXTURE & TYPE:
MEDIUM
STRAIGHT

FIRST LOOK

Anne has the perfect combo of medium texture with medium density. Although straight, her hair holds whatever curl I put in. She has hair with memory!

1 Starting with wet hair, blow-dry hair smooth.

2 Start at the top of the head and spray with heat-protector spray setting lotion.

3 Heat top section of hair with the flat iron.

4 Roll large Velcro rollers along the top section. Secure each roller with a metal clip to hold.

5 Wrap Velcro at the base with facial tissue if you have fine hair to avoid breaking the hair.

6 Continue heating and applying rollers, working from the back of the head to the sides. Use larger jumbo rollers for the back of the head.

7 For the sides, make two big sections and roll them under.

8 Spray the whole head with hair spray.

9 Use a blow dryer on each roller to reheat the set up a little (if you want).

10 Leave the set in as long as possible then brush out.

MEDIUM
STRAIGHT

SECOND LOOK

For her second look, I decided to bring out Anne's wild, luxurious side. Bet you wouldn't think from her "before" photo that Anne's hair could look like this! Just shows you what a good curling iron can do. Who wouldn't love silky, sumptuous hair like this?

1. Section off the hair. Make a horizontal parting, splitting the side section into two sections.

2. Spiral hair around a curling iron, using the full barrel of the iron. Curl away from the face.

3. Wind hair away from the face on a diagonal.

4. Use a metal clip to secure the curls.

5. Moving to the back of the head, section off a 2-inch (5 cm) section at the nape.

6. Pin the rest of the hair up at the crown.

7. Take diagonal 2-inch (5 cm) sections, working from the side and winding the hair toward the center of the head.

Bring down the next 2-inch (5 cm) section from the pinned-up hair at the crown. Work through each larger section, creating smaller workable sections until all the hair is curled, moving in toward the middle of the back of the head.

8. Roll the last top section at the top of the crown under toward the back of the head, spiraling the hair along the iron.

9. If the result is too tight, you can use a bigger-barreled iron to create a larger curl/wave pattern.

10. Brush through the curls with a boar-bristle paddle brush to create waves. Use a wide-tooth comb to backcomb and spread the waves.

11. Use a little hair spray to finish.

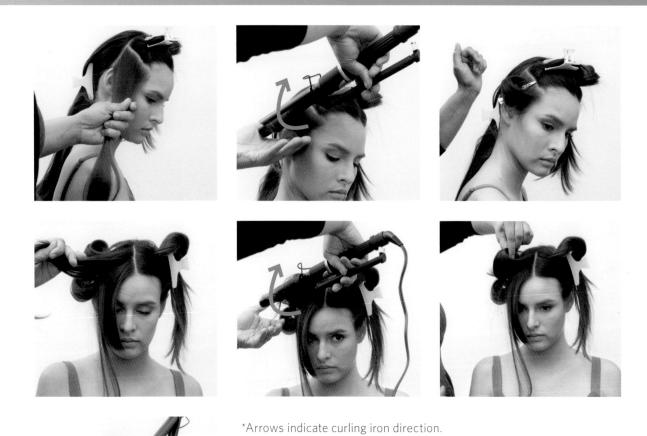

*Arrows indicate curling iron direction.

HAIR TEXTURE & TYPE:
MEDIUM STRAIGHT

THIRD LOOK

For a slinky, sophisticated evening look, I gave Anne a deep side part and curled her luxuriant tresses so they fell in a silken sweep down one side. This look focuses attention on her beautiful features first, then on the gorgeous sweep of her hair.

1 Section off the hair. Make a horizontal parting, splitting the side section into two sections.

2 Spiral hair around a curling iron, using the full barrel of the iron. Curl away from the face.

3 Wind hair away from the face on a diagonal.

4 Use a metal clip to secure the curls.

5 Moving to the back of the head, section off a 2-inch (5 cm) section at the nape.

6 Pin the rest of the hair up at the crown.

7 Take diagonal 2-inch (5 cm) sections, working from the side and winding the hair toward the center of the head.

Bring down the next 2-inch (5 cm) section from the pinned-up hair at the crown. Work through each larger section, creating smaller workable sections until all the hair is curled, moving in toward the middle of the back of the head.

8 Roll the last top section at the top of the crown under toward the back of the head, spiraling the hair along the iron.

9 If the result is too tight, you can use a bigger-barreled iron to create a larger curl/wave pattern.

10 Make a low side part and brush hair smooth to create sleek waves.

SMOOTHING CREAM FOR THE FINISHING TOUCH

You may want to use some smoothing cream for this look. It will help keep the curls connected and flowing into a wave pattern.

«REMEMBER,
— a wave is JUST —
A CURL brushed OUT!»

*Arrows indicate curling iron direction.

COLOUR-TREATED
MEDIUM

FARRIS

Farris's classic look is timeless. On her colour-treated hair, I took extra care with leave-in conditioners to keep her hair at its best.

HAIR TEXTURE & TYPE:

COLOUR-TREATED MEDIUM

FIRST LOOK

Farris's classic look is timeless. On her colour-treated hair, I took extra care with leave-in conditioners to keep her hair at its best. From sexy to sophisticated, Farris can do it all!

1. Start by spritzing the hair with water to dampen. Apply leave-in conditioner.

2. Begin creating the style by sectioning in the back at the nape. Use a large, round brush to smooth with the blow dryer.

3. Blow hair straight and smooth.

4. Use a flat iron to smooth the sections.

5. Section off hair from the crown to behind the ears. Brush and use (dry) aerosol hair spray to prep. Make a ponytail.

6. Create a low side part. Use spray and comb to smooth the front and side sections.

7. Curl big sections of the ends of the hair for a curved shape. This will create a curled-under wave pattern. Work your way around the face, curling sections under. Curl ponytail under as well.

8. For the left side: Pull left (or lighter) side back. Smooth and wrap around ponytail base. Secure with a hairpin to hold in place.

9. For the right side: Brush hair smooth, pull over, and wind around the base of the ponytail. Secure with a hairpin.

10. Split the ponytail into two sections. Use a wide-tooth comb to backcomb hair in each section.

11. Smooth each section. Roll, twist, and pin into place next to ponytail base.

12. Break up and spread the two rolled sections to create a loose bun.

VARIATION:
Unpin the sections of hair and backcomb them, creating more texture and volume. Twist and pin the sections into place.

COLOUR-TREATED MEDIUM

SECOND LOOK

Farris's second look is looser than the first look, but is still sleek and sophisticated. A discreet ponytail confines the hair subtly at the nape, keeping the visual focus on the deep wave in front. I call this style a "soft wave with a side pony wrap."

1. Brush back section over to behind the right ear and pull into a ponytail.

2. Curl side sections down and toward the face with a narrow curling iron. The front section also should be curled toward the face.

3. For the top section, curl diagonal partings down and away from the face.

4. Curl the ponytail one section at a time.

5. Apply texture cream gel through curled strands.

6. Brush or comb (depending on the hair texture) through the wavy curls.

7. Comb front section so wave pattern becomes more defined and uniform.

8. Finger-comb heavy side section and then wrap around base of ponytail. Pin into place at the back base of ponytail.

9. Take the other side section and pull back to ponytail base. Wrap it around base and pin into place.

10. Backcomb the ponytail really well. Smooth ponytail with hands and comb a little bit. Twist or roll up into a ball shape. Pin into place.

11. Use comb and fingers to fine-tune waves.

HAIR TEXTURE & TYPE:
COLOUR-TREATED
MEDIUM

THIRD LOOK

With this look, Farris lets down her hair to create sensuous waves and a come-hither look. The deep off-center part draws the eye to the sleek, shiny sweep of hair across the top of the head before it's irresistibly drawn to those gorgeous waves.

1 Brush out waves.

2 Wrap a section of hair in a semicircle around the crown of the head. Pin up and away.

3 Attach single-layer hair track under parting at occipital bone.

4 Blend with fingers and brush.

5 Curl hair away from face with small curling iron. Spiral hair in vertical sections around the head.

6 Brush through curls to create waves.

7 Backcomb with a large-tooth comb to create fullness and uniformity of the waves.

CHANGING THE PART

Here's a quick way to change a part: Use a liquid spray gel and blow dryer, and comb to create a new direction for the part.

HAIR TEXTURE & TYPE:
COLOUR-TREATED
MEDIUM

FOURTH LOOK

Farris's fourth look is a more windblown, less restrained version of the third style. I've abandoned all traces of vintage starlet, but with that angel face, there will always be a trace of innocence shining through!

1 Brush out waves.

2 Wrap a section of hair in a semicircle around the crown of the head. Pin up and away.

3 Attach single-layer hair track under parting at occipital bone.

4 Blend with fingers and brush.

5 Curl hair away from face with small curling iron. Spiral hair in vertical sections around the head.

6 Brush through curls to create waves.

7 Use a large-tooth comb to backcomb and separate the curl to create more voluminous waves. Brush away from the face.

«THE *basic steps* FOR THIS LOOK
— *are the same as for* —
FARRIS'S THIRD LOOK.
BUT WHAT A DIFFERENCE
THAT FINAL BACKCOMBING MAKES!»

TO LOOSEN CURLS

The more you brush, the

looser the curl will become!

KAREN

I took Karen's hair from good
to great with a bob and a
face-flattering style.

MEDIUM
wavy
COLOUR-TREATED

I TOOK KAREN'S HAIR from good to great with a bob and a face-flattering style. Look how much healthier her hair looks now that the ends are smooth and even. And what a difference bangs can make!

HOLD THAT RAZOR!

Be careful to not use the razor with curly and/or wavy hair and colour-treated hair. It distorts the hair.

First Step: The Cut

[1] Towel-dry hair.

[2] Cut the line on the back of the head at the jawline.

[3] Keep the front layers.

[4] Cut the bob so the bottom line meets the sides at the middle (point cutting). Do not blunt-cut.

[5] Go around the bottom perimeter with thinning shears to lighten the line.

Second Step: Styling

[1] Don't use any styling product (yet).

[2] Blow-dry smooth. Keep the dryer pointed down and use a large, round brush.

[3] Blow the left front forward from the side part.

[4] Run texturizing paste through hair.

[5] Use a tourmaline round brush and blower to smooth and finish ends.

[6] Blow fringe flipped up and back.

[7] Redirect the part.

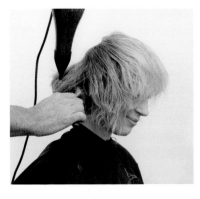

Marcelin

Marcelin's gorgeous hair just screamed for the red-carpet treatment. Her beauty speaks for itself, so I kept the styles simple and classically elegant.

HAIR TEXTURE & TYPE:
wavy
THICK

FIRST LOOK

A chignon and gardenia (silk, in this case) transform Marcelin into a diva in her first look.

Cover Shot

1. Apply leave-in conditioner.

2. Blow hair smooth with big round brush.

3. Smooth hair with flat iron.

4. Spritz a tiny amount of water on hair to get all the little hairs in place as you brush the hair back into a low ponytail.

5. Split ponytail into 3 sections.

6. Start with the side sections first. Use texture cream—apply to one section at a time and twist.

7. Keep twisting one section at a time. The section will start to twist up into a coil as you twist it.

8. Allow the coil to twist up and secure it near the base of the ponytail. Secure with bobby pins.

9. Apply cream to last (middle) section and gather all the hair cleanly. Twist and coil up to base and secure with pins.

10. Position and place hair ornament flower. Secure with pin.

wavy
THICK

SECOND LOOK

Giving Marcelin a contemporary style for her second look, I loosened the bun, making it a little wilder, and replaced the flower with a headband with a barrette. Looser, yes, but every bit as elegant. It's a real red-carpet look!

Red Carpet

1. Secure hair in a low ponytail.

2. Curl with small curling iron.

3. Backcomb with a comb.

4. Gather hair into a messy bun.

5. Adjust shape of bun and secure with pins.

6. Spray with hair spray.

7. Attach headband.

« It just takes
— *a little diamond flash* —
TO ADD GLAM ELEGANCE

TO A SIMPLE STYLE. »

«THESE styles
— *are easy* —
AND FRESH. »

BALANCING WITH BANDS

A pretty headband is just the formal touch you need to make an informal style like a messy bun look intentional, not sloppy. When you add that headband, it takes this look from good to great.

FINE
wavy

NANCY

Adding a long fringe and smoothing and shaping Nancy's hair took her from hot to red hot in a heartbeat.

FINE
wavy

FIRST LOOK

Adding a long fringe and smoothing and shaping Nancy's hair took her from cute to red hot in a heartbeat. What do you think?

LIGHTWEIGHT BODY

Using a dry shampoo on fine hair is a great way to add body without weighing your hair down.

To prep Nancy for styling, I first gave her a haircut. I cut the ends in back and reshaped the front with a long fringe to frame Nancy's jaw line. Then we were ready to style.

1. Divide hair into 3 sections: middle part; part from crown to behind ears; and back section.

2. Part off a small section at the nape.

3. Blow-dry with a large, round brush, moving under the hair.

4. Blow-dry front forward and under.

5. To create volume on top, take a large top section and use a flat iron to heat up the section.

6. Wind a jumbo Velcro roller toward the back of head, dragging the roller forward and over. Direct it so the roller sits squarely on its base.

7. Top it off with a spritz of hair spray.

8. Leave the roller in as long as possible.

9. Backcomb at the root on the crown and top of the head.

10. Spray hair spray on backcombed hair.

11. Use a round brush to blow more fullness into the fringe area, and also blow out the back, combing to smooth and blend. Use fingers to blend more if needed.

12. Use a little powder dry colour shampoo at the roots.

13. Finish ends with a 1-inch (25 mm) barrel curling iron, curling back and away from the face.

14. Use your fingers and a comb to finish the look, with the front pieces moving away from the face and fringe moving to one side.

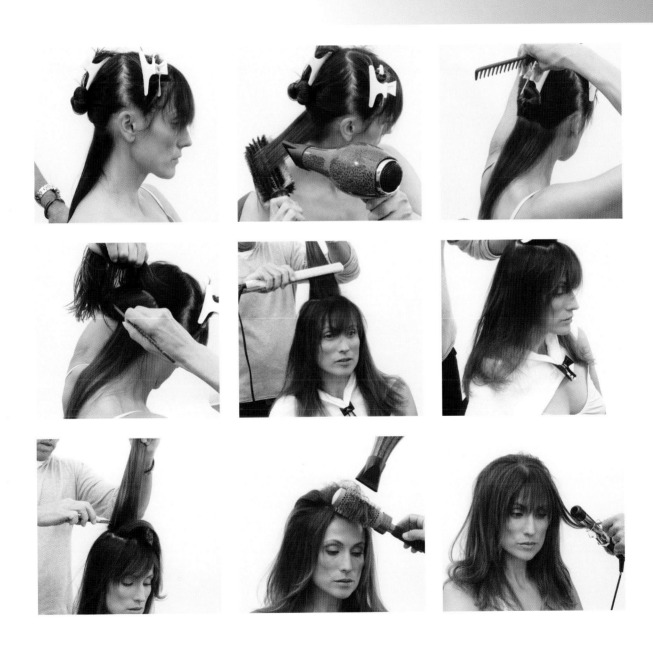

HAIR TEXTURE & TYPE:
FINE
wavy

SECOND LOOK

A strong jaw and classic features like Nancy's deserve to be highlighted, and I did just that for her second look by pulling her hair back. The ponytail gives a touch of schoolgirl freshness and freedom, while still screaming high style.

1. Backcomb at the roots.

2. Gather hair back with your hands for a messy ponytail. Secure with a covered band.

3. Take a small section of ponytail and wrap around the covered band. Pin into place under ponytail base.

4. To get a cleaner neckline, grab hair from back of neck (nape) and pull toward covered band. Use a bobby pin to pin hair in place under band.

5. Curl sections of ponytail with 1-inch (25 mm) curling iron.

6. Use hair spray to clean up hair strands, moving toward the covered band.

THICK
DENSE
curly

Jen

Jen has massive, insane amounts of hair. I literally had my hands full! Straightening Jen's hair allowed me to update her style to a sleeker, more sophisticated look.

THICK
DENSE
curly

JEN HAS MASSIVE, insane amounts of hair. I literally had my hands full! Straightening Jen's hair allowed me to update her style to a sleeker, more sophisticated look.

1. Make four basic sections: Part down the middle; part from the crown to behind the ears.

2. Take a small, 1-inch (2.5 cm) wide horizontal section down and across at the nape of the neck.

3. Take a small, 1 x 1-inch (2.5 x 2.5 cm) section from that section. Spray a light mist of water on the section.

4. Use the wet-to-dry flat iron to smooth and straighten the hair. Take smaller or larger sections, depending on how thick your hair is.

5. Take sections, starting in the front, and curl sections away from the face with a large curling iron.

6. Use a brush to shape the style.

HOW TO USE A FLAT IRON

Remember that sectioning the hair makes life more manageable and ensures that you will get the best results when using a flat iron or any heat-styling tool. Always divide your hair into big sections first. Then take smaller sections from each big section when you work with the heat tools.

Use a comb to comb through your hair as you use the flat iron. This will ensure that the hair doesn't tangle as you slide the iron down the shaft of the hair section. Also, it will keep you from burning your fingers after the iron has smoothed out the curl or wave. Blisters are not fun!

«JEN SHOWS how easy it is
to do it yourself
— if you know what you're doing!

Always take it STEP BY STEP.»

FINE
DENSE
curly

DIANA

I love how natural Diana looks! All I wanted to do was freshen up that look.

HAIR TEXTURE & TYPE:

FINE
DENSE
curly

I LOVE HOW NATURAL Diana looks! All I wanted to do was freshen up her look.

Cut, Style, and Set

1 I cut a few inches off the length.

2 Next, I cut a frame around the face.

3 I started the layers at her chin and pulled everything forward, resulting in a long, layered effect.

Next, the style:

1 Apply leave-in cream conditioner and silicone.

2 Section off hair from the bottom in the back.

3 Use large, round brush to blow hair smooth and straight, turning it under.

4 Sides: Section off from the bottom in 2-inch (5 cm) horizontal partings. Roll hair under while drying and then flip the ends back away from the face.

5 Dry side sections down from the top of the head.

6 Front: Blow sections forward toward the face.

7 Hairline: Use the heat from the dryer with a comb at the hairline to smooth hair from the roots.

8 When the whole head is finished, apply more leave-in conditioner.

The Hot Roller Set

1 Roll sides back away from the face in one big section.

2 Divide the back into two big sections, rolled back toward the middle of the head. Roll front section away from the face.

3 Allow the rollers to set, then brush out curls.

4 Use blow dryer to soften the curls using fingers and silicone.

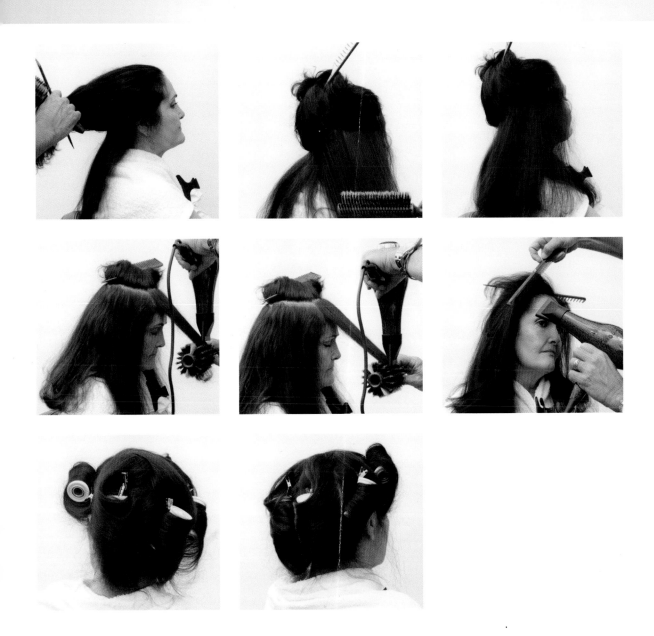

APPENDIX

ROBERT'S ESSENTIAL Styling KIT

I'VE DISCUSSED THE TOOLS of my trade in detail in chapters 3, 4, and 5 of this book. But I wanted to make sure you had a list in one convenient place, so you can photocopy it and take it with you to the store if you want.

LARGE ROUND BRUSH: Important tool for smoothing and straightening the hair with a blow dryer.

STYLING BRUSH (FLAT PADDLE BRUSH): Great for styling updos and brushing and smoothing the hair.

LARGE-TOOTH COMB: Great for backcombing.

CURLING IRONS: Used to create curl and waves.

FLAT IRON: Used to straighten hair and also heat sections of hair when using Velcro rollers in certain situations.

BLOW DRYER: 'Nuff said.

COVERED ELASTIC BANDS: Always use a covered elastic band when creating ponytails. They will protect your hair from ripping and damage that regular elastic bands cause.

ELASTIC BANDS: Great for creating a ponytail on really thick hair. Gather the hair together and hook one end of the bungie where the base of the ponytail will be. Wrap the bungie around the hair until secure and hook to the side of ponytail.

BARRETTES: Used for accent and styling.

ALLIGATOR CLAMPS: Used to hold large hair sections in place.

HAIRPINS: Horseshoe-shaped pins used to secure updos.

BOBBY PINS: Used for updos. Does anyone in the world NOT know what a bobby pin is?!

VELCRO ROLLERS: Create volume, wave, and in some cases, curl.

HOT ROLLERS: For the set.

HAIR SPRAY: Indispensable. Use the aerosol, not the pump.

LEAVE-IN CONDITIONER: Restores moisture; also good as a styling tool.

SILICONE SERUM: Defrizzes, rescues split ends, and seals extremely dry hair.

HEAT-PROTECTOR SPRAY: Use with a curling iron. Protects the hair from heat damage and helps set the curl.

HAIR EXTENSIONS: Add length, weight, and bulk to natural hair.

COLORED DRY (POWDER) SHAMPOO: To cover gray temporarily. Sometimes used to give the hair texture at the roots when applying extensions.

ACKNowledgMENTS

When this book idea was presented to me, I had no idea what it would entail. (What was I thinking?!)

I am humbled by the support that surrounded me during this whole process. To say that it has brought me to tears at times is an understatement. Everywhere I turned along the way, an angel was there offering his/her support.

No great beauty photograph can exist without a great photographer. I am fortunate to have as my friend, and part of my family, the amazingly talented Alberto Tolot. His photographs in this book speak for themselves. His approach to photography is effortless and awe inspiring. He is a master.

Alberto's wife, Francesca Tolot—a master in her own right and an inspiration to makeup artists worldwide—has also added her talent to *Fabulous Hair*. Her continual support as a collaborator and as a best friend is one of the most profound relationships in my life. I love and thank you both from the bottom of my heart.

Thanks also to Cristiano Tolot, the son of Alberto and Francesca, for the cover design.

Robert Jones is a talented and giving soul. The fact that his makeup has graced the women of these pages is just the icing on the cake. His gentle spirit helped guide this book to its end and his experience in writing three successful makeup books provided me with the support and guidance I needed during the times when I felt like I had no idea what I was doing. Thank you Beck, I love you.

Robert was also responsible for my introduction to Fair Winds Press and to my publisher, Will Kiester. I think this was a good thing (kidding, Will!)! It was a great experience and the team at Fair Winds is outstanding: Amanda Waddell, Daria Perreault, John Gettings, my art director Rosalind Wanke, my editor Ellen Phillips, and designer Carol Holtz. And a special thank you to Ken Fund for all his support. You all did an amazing job—thank you for your passion and support.

Salma Salma Salma. Wow. As much as I have tried to keep this book far from the celebrity-driven madness that we see every day and focus on the principles of hairdressing, there is no way of me getting around the fact that it is the world in which I live and work. I love it and to have my friend, the beautiful and talented Salma Hayek, grace the cover of my book is a gift beyond my expectations. To know her as I do is to know a woman of great strength, passion, and joie de vivre. It is not just a beautiful face that makes for a beautiful woman, make no mistake about it. Without the heart to match, you will never see beauty's true potential. Salma epitomizes this. Chucha, I love you.

Debra, my dear, sweet, gentle, beautiful, funny Debra. Wow, can you believe this? Thank you, my loyal friend. Your kind and heartfelt words will remind me always of your loyalty and friendship. I am so grateful for you in my life.

And to all the famous, talented women who gave of their time and heart and wrote such beautiful words about me. I am, as always, at your service! Thank you.

To the others, who are to me famous, legendary, and talented, without whom my life would be a little less perfect. Your endorsements are so very humbling.

Special thanks to Paul Starr, my friend. I will miss you.

Thanks to my team:
Robert Jones, makeup

Nancy La Scala, actress/model/producer/best friend/can do anything

Kenny Wujek, the best

Aviva Perea, my assistant, I love you (Look out for Aviva!)

Kathleena Gorga, you have no idea!

Rosalind Wanke, art director darling

Alberto Tolot

Ed Cawas, digital tech

Peter Cavolatos, step-by-step photographer

You all did more than I could ever have imagined. Thank you.

My agents Lisa Walker and Samer Fawaz. I love you and thank you for understanding how crazy I can be. I love you both.

Adir, you are heaven sent and you know why, and the same for Cari Ross, who persuaded me to go further.

Anne Hardy, my publicist, thank you thank you thank you.

Judith Regan, you are the best, thank you for your guidance and passion.

Jamie Glassman for the BeBe connection. And BeBe, for lending us all the clothes for the book. It was amazing and everyone fit the sample sizes, honest!

To Michael Elliot of Smashbox Studios for his generosity.

Special thanks to Staci Peterson and Terri Morgan, friends from the past who flew from Seattle so I could have their beautiful faces in my book (and for reminding me that you can go back and how good it is)!

Matthew Van Leeuwen for Salma's insane makeup for the cover. And Jewels for pulling all the amazing clothes together (sorry, baby, that you don't see your work but you were great!).

I could never even guess how many heads of hair I have touched in my long career but you know if you are out there and we have had the pleasure of working together. Remember that each of you are just as important to me today as you were the day I saw you.

Carol Perry, Diane Peterson, and Julie Hassler, thank you for sitting through those three and four hour haircuts. See, it was worth it and I will never forget it!

Thank you to my mother, Barbara Vetica, who never stopped me from baking cakes and watching her do her makeup and letting me do those Thursday night redos. I know it was tough raising eight kids. I love you Mom.

And to Dolly D'Andrea, for always providing me a safe haven as I grew older, when my world was turned upside down. I love you.

I lost my father this past year. He left a great legacy: eight children, twenty-plus grandchildren, and three great grandchildren. He instilled in us a sense of purpose, strength, and pride. I will forever be in his shadow—and I am proud to be there.

And finally, Giorgio Bosso, my partner in life, the love of my life, my soul mate. It is you that I give the most gratitude. To love is a gift, to be loved unconditionally is a blessing. You never stop inspiring me.

ALBERTO TOLOT was born in Italy near the city of Venice where he was a professional musician and sometimes photographer. In the city of Milan his hobby of photography grew to a profession, and in 1983 he moved to Los Angeles. Since then he has worked for numerous magazines, record companies, and advertising clients. Alberto has photographed some of the world's most beautiful women, including Julia Roberts, Angelina Jolie, Halle Berry, Sharon Stone, Kim Basinger, Madonna, Elizabeth Taylor, and Barbra Streisand. In addition to his editorial work, Alberto is in the process of publishing a book of his photographs and personal work.

ALBERTO
TOLOT

His client list includes celebrities such as Renée Zellweger, Mariah Carey, Avril Lavigne, Naomi Watts, Eva Longoria, Debra Messing, Shakira, Salma Hayek, and Hilary Swank. His work has also been featured in countless magazines, music videos, ad campaigns, and red carpet events.

Robert began his career in Italy, where he quickly established himself with Italy's top fashion publications, including *Vogue*, *Harper's Bazaar*, *Amica*, and *Elle*. He then returned to the States and took Hollywood by storm. His unique and innovative approach to hair design quickly elevated him to an elite status working with the best of the best. Robert continues to set the standard for hair today. He lives in Los Angeles.

ABOUT THE author